YOU'VE GOT THE MONEY

Rebuilding the Rural Bridge to the Global Economy

YOU'VE GOT THE MONEY
Rebuilding the Rural Bridge to the Global Economy

Copyright © 2012 by Fred Hiner

ISBN: -13: 978-1508675228

ISBN-10: 1508675228

Sere Administrative Services
President - Fred Hiner
17330 W Center RD Omaha, NE 68130
Tel - 888 527 0773 ~ Fax - 888 527 0773
Email: info@sereas.org
Website: sereas.org

Printed in the United States of America

10 9 8 7 6 5 4 3 2 1

YOU'VE GOT THE MONEY

Rebuilding the Rural Bridge to the Global Economy

Fred Hiner

DEDICATION

R URAL AMERICA IS a place where I found trust, love, and real people. When I was thirteen years old, my father was shot twice in the head and killed. As a child growing up, some of my family was very divided—and crazy, if you ask me. With multiple divorces, stepsiblings, and no understanding of why I was alive, I had not yet really seen a normal family or been in a normal family environment when my dad was shot.

While being processed into the witness protection program, I was sent to a farm. I did not know these people, but it was not a choice. When I met the family that was going to take care of me, I almost laughed aloud. They were very kind, but they dressed funny. The old men wore overhauls; the young men looked like their mommas had dressed them, and it seemed as though they were okay with it, so as usual, I just tried to fit in.

My first day on the farm, I felt like I was some kind of soldier, because I learned that I was expected to work. Work was something that I was not afraid of but did not expect. I thought these people were going to feel sorry for me—and all that dumb stuff—but boy, was I wrong. I remember when it was time for dinner, the old screen door just kept flying open. The neighbors and family members were just coming on in and sitting down for dinner—and they were ready to eat!

I had never seen a family dinner like this one. Everyone was so welcome, and family or not, it was as if you were. It was like a dream come true for me. The food was better than from a restaurant; the people at the table were nicer than nice and full of love. Wow, what an experience this turned out to be. It immediately began to build trust in my heart and that was something that I had never had. I learned how to milk cows, bail hay, and the neighbor kids took me coon hunting. Now that was a real treat; that is until they said I needed to go up in that tree and run that coon out of it. Yup, you know the rest of that story—the coon ran *me* out of the tree.

When the neighbors needed help with the business of their farm, we just helped them and did not charge them a penny. What a concept. I believe Rural America is the Identity and Morality of this Great Nation.

With Adopt a Model™ system, SERE Administrative Services can assist you with a customized bridge for your community. It addresses the agricultural, manufacturing, education, business, cultural, and green issues that are relative to your specific need. This bridge is a partnership for rural America to the metro and global economy. With a holistic approach to economic development, you can maximize your existing resources, increase the quality of living, and develop long-range sustainability to a healthy and wealthy community.

I want to dedicate this book to my awesome wife, Jennifer, and my three perfect children, Micaiah, Micah, and Moriah, who let me give a portion of my life and make sacrifices to let me build the model for rural America.

To my Friend and Mentor, Jesus Christ. To Jean Boles and Everett O'Keefe for helping me to edit and focus, and to Harry Truman.

I have written this book and built my company as a token of honor for what people in Rural America did to help me. Rural America is full of kind, loving, and real people. So, please enjoy the rest of this book, and I hope it works for you.

About the Author

Fred Hiner is a family man, married to his sweetheart, Jennifer for sixteen years. They have three children: Micaiah, Micah, and Moriah. Fred believes the secret to his success is a strong marriage and accepting the role of being a supportive and engaged father. Spending valuable time with his spouse and children has allowed Fred to exercise his abilities in the corporate world, to work guilt-free and to see the desired results from his efforts.

Mr. Hiner has consulted thousands of families from small businesses and small towns. His macroeconomic passion has opened doors around the world through sharing his insights on restoring the family. His deep perception into proper building methods has achieved results from socio-economic impacts to industry revolutions. Mr. Hiner has offered free business and marriage counseling for the past fifteen years, and one of his clients became his best friend. Practicing every ounce of the teachings with wisdom, Shawn Nelson says, "It changed my family and my business; now he is my best friend."

"How you run your home, is how you will run your business," Hiner teaches. This concept has affected many who have come to get business advice and who are told to change the home and business success will follow. "If you want to make a difference, start at home."

CONTENTS

DEDICATION v

About the Author ix

CHAPTER ONE 13

    Build A Bridge... 13

CHAPTER TWO 29

    Have A Blueprint... 29

CHAPTER THREE 49

    Invest in People 49

CHAPTER FOUR.. 69

    A Band-Aid Won't Work 69

CHAPTER FIVE 79

    Build A Team.. 79

CHAPTER SIX.. 107

    Go Fish.. 107

INDEX 122

CHAPTER ONE

Build A Bridge

A S A BRIDGE THAT remains intact, connected by massive and many cables, a strong foundation and a solid architectural design—Adopt a Model™ sustains the community when it faces strong economic winds and storms. Depending upon the organizational obstacles, the demographic divide and the depth of debt, it determines the type of bridge needed in rural development and a struggling community. Whether it is a creek, stream, river, lake, or a bay, we need bridges to facilitate proper transportation of goods and services. Likewise, a small covered bridge over a creek in a rural area represents a local flower business, or a suspension bridge over a bay represents an industrial park that is no longer used to its greatest potential. Innovative development is necessary to sustain growth and create a demand for products.

Before you can decide what type of bridge to build, rebuild or repair, you need to know what obstacles are preventing its completion and success. What challenges are you currently facing? What are the problems that have failed in the past? What types of issues are outdated, preventing you from remaining competitive?

On September 15, 2011, President Obama delivered a political address for his new jobs' bill saying that there were 153 structurally deficient bridges in North Carolina that are on the verge of collapse and need to be repaired or replaced. However, under federal guidelines, the DOT inspectors examine North Carolina's 17,000 bridges at least every two years. As it turns out, it was reported that about 2,700 bridges in the US are rated below federal standards as "structural deficient".[1]

As of September 2009, there were a reported 507,961 bridges in the United States.[2] In 2008, the U.S. Bridge Statistics reported that there were 151,171 bridges in urban areas and 448,595 in rural.[3] The same can be said for *financial bridges* in the economy. Small business comprises 99.7% of all employers and provides 50% of jobs in the United States. In fact, small business provides 66% of jobs in rural communities.[4]

---

[1] http://www.beaufortobserver.net/Articles-c-2011-09-20-255827.112112-Of-bridges-and-taxes-What-Obama-says-is-simply-not-true.html
[2] http://www.betterroads.com/category/bridge-inventory/erroads.randallreillycms.com/files/ 2009/11/BR1109_BridgeInventory.pdf
[3] http://www.infrastructurereportcard.org/fact-sheet/bridges (Transportation Statistics Annual Report, U.S. Department of Transportation, Bureau of Transportation Statistics, 2008).
[4] http://www.nsba.biz/vote/70_MAV_Factsheet.pdf

In the Adopt a Model™ program, "bridges" represent the economical conduit to local businesses along with corporations and the consumer. The great financial decline and the business dilemma remain because no one is inspecting the *bridges* in rural America.

Decay in our trade and industry bridges have prevented businesses from crossing because no one is sure that bridges will hold them. Therefore, no one is crossing the bridge. There is more money in banks today than in history, but it's not moving. Bank of America, while shrinking its assets and loan portfolio, has $172 billion in cash on its balance sheets. Citibank is shrinking on $185 billion in cash. JP Morgan Chase has $72 billion, yet just try to get a loan from any one of them—not going to happen.[5]

The questions remain: Is the economy failing? Is America out of money? Are you waiting on a "bail out" to restore or create new jobs in your community? Do you have the support system in place to revive your city or state? No? Then the Adopt a Model™ program is for you—you just do not have the proper bridges in place to stimulate growth and economic transportation.

Overcome Obstacles

When it comes to making the bridge a reality, it seems like an impossible task. Obstacles challenge its success from the beginning to the end. Consider a brilliant feat of 19th-century engineering; the Brooklyn Bridge was a bridge of

---

[5] http://www.nytimes.com/2010/09/12/opinion/12bove.html

many firsts. It was the first suspension bridge to use steel for its cable wire. It was the first bridge to use explosives in a dangerous underwater device called a *caisson*. At the time it was built, the 3,460-foot Brooklyn Bridge was also crowned the longest suspension bridge in the world.

Picture Collection, The Branch Libraries,
The New York Public Library.

But the Brooklyn Bridge was plagued with its share of problems. Talk of somehow bridging the East River began as early as 1800, when large bridges were essentially dreams. The advantages of having a convenient link between the two growing cities of New York and Brooklyn were obvious. However, the idea was thought to be impossible because of the width of the waterway, which despite its name wasn't really a river. The East River is actually a salt-water estuary, prone to turbulence and tidal conditions.

Further complicating matters was the fact that the East River was one of the busiest waterways on earth, with hundreds of crafts of all sizes sailing on it at any time. (Sounds like an economic board in the middle of elections.) Any bridge spanning the water would have to allow ships to pass beneath it, meaning a suspension bridge was the only practical solution.[6]

Before construction even began, the bridge's chief engineer, John A. Roebling, sustained a crush injury to his foot while conducting surveys for the bridge project when a ferry pinned it against a piling. After the amputation of his crushed toes, he developed a tetanus infection and soon resulted in his death.[7] His son, Washington Roebling, took over the project. Three years later, Washington developed a crippling illness called Caisson's Disease, known today as "the bends." Bedridden, but determined to stay in charge, Roebling used a telescope to keep watch over the bridge's progress. He dictated instructions to his wife, Emily, who passed on his orders to the workers. During this time, an unexpected blast wrecked one caisson, a fire damaged another, and a cable snapped from its anchorage and crashed into the river.

The building of the bridge was always controversial, and not just because skeptics thought Roebling's design was unsafe. There were stories of political payoffs and corruption, rumors of carpet bags stuffed with cash being given to characters like New York's "Boss" Tweed. Of course, that was the old days. Right?

---

[6] http://history1800s.about.com/od/bridgebuilding/a/brooklynbrid01.htm

[7] http://en.wikipedia.org/wiki/Brooklyn_Bridge

In one famous case, a manufacturer of wire rope sold inferior material to the bridge company. The shady contractor escaped prosecution. But the bad wire he sold is still in the bridge, as it couldn't be removed once it was worked into the cables. Washington Roebling compensated for its presence, making sure the inferior material wouldn't affect the strength of the bridge.[8]

Despite these problems, construction continued at a feverish pace. By 1883, 14 years after it began, Roebling successfully guided the completion of one of the most famous bridges in the world—without ever leaving his apartment.

On opening day, 150,300 people crossed the bridge. One week after the opening on May 30, 1883, a rumor that the Bridge was going to collapse caused a stampede, which crushed and killed at least twelve people.[9] On May 17, 1884, P. T. Barnum helped to squelch doubts about the bridge's stability—while publicizing his famous circus— when one of his most famous attractions, Jumbo, led a parade of 21 elephants over the Brooklyn Bridge.[10] Today, the Brooklyn Bridge is the second busiest bridge in New

---

[8] http://history1800s.about.com/od/bridgebuilding/a/brooklynbrid01. htm

[9] "Died on the New Bridge: Fatal Crush at the Western Approach". *The New York Times*. May 31, 1883.

[10] *Twenty-One Elephants*, Phil Bildner (New York: Simon & Schuster, 2004).

York City. One hundred forty-four thousand vehicles cross the bridge every day.[11]

The Brooklyn Bridge is 3,460 feet long and cost about $15 million to build and approximately 27 persons died during its construction.[12] Building an economic bridge equally faces its own challenges and requires certain prerequisites in order to overcome the challenges in developing growth, sustainability, and positioning rural America for future demand. Rural areas, dependent upon single industries for their livelihood and well-being, have bankrupt many towns and communities in rural America. Rural areas have not had the resources of a diverse economy and a broad-based social infrastructure to make the necessary adjustments.

With rising energy prices, restrictions upon credit, a U.S. grain embargo, a demand for oil and other energy resources in the world market, and heightened foreign competition from third world countries, the recession of the 1980s had a far greater impact upon rural areas than urban ones. As a result, unemployment in rural areas skyrocketed, wages and salaries grew at a much slower pace, and rural poverty increased rapidly.

With the decline of U.S. manufacturing, such as the auto industry, textiles, clothing, and leathergoods, the severity of the economic downturn in rural areas began to spin out of control. The loss of manufacturing jobs was not temporary

---

[11] http://www.pbs.org/wgbh/buildingbig/wonder/structure/brooklyn.html

[12] http://history1800s.about.com/od/bridgebuilding/a/brooklyn brid01.htm

setbacks; they were permanent. The disappearance of industrial factors placed (non-skilled labor) individuals at risk for employment.

Not only was there a paradigm shift in employee skills, the centralized American banking industries shifted their investments from "locally owned banks to main offices of state and regional banks," making it nearly impossible for rural residents to obtain a business loan. Thus, as credit markets became globalized, and investment decisions more detached from local communities, lenders increasingly turned away from rural investments in favor of larger and more profitable investments in the international credit market.

Rural communities were now consider a "high risk" and posed a capital risk to creditors. Venture capitalists frowned upon the "low standard" business plans and financial information presented in their proposals, which was now a common practice in a loan application— typically used as a screening device for financial institutions.

A mismatch between the qualities of the rural labor force and the needs of a diversified and information-intensive economy constitutes an obstacle to holistic development. The skills of factory workers, farmers, and miners do not correspond to the needs of the growing service sector of high-tech manufacturing. But retraining these workers for jobs that do not exist does little good either.

Another obstacle is location. Distance from urban centers and small, dispersed populations characterize rural areas. The distance from urban areas limits access to employment, goods, and services. This raises the transportation costs involved in buying or selling products in rural areas. At the same time, the small populations of rural areas diminish their ability to produce goods or services cheaply because they typically cannot achieve the economies of scale that reduce the unit cost of production.

The nature, the number, and the severity of the obstacles facing rural communities vary widely. The diversity of the communities requires a variety of strategies for development. These strategies should address the underlying symptoms of distress and generate sustainable solutions. Rural areas need the proper infrastructure to survive in today's economic challenges. They need a *bridge* to compete with urban and metro competition.

Support Your Bridge with Towers

The Brooklyn Bridge featured two arched portals: 276-foot neo-Gothic granite towers built to withstand strong winds and provide support for rail lines. The towers were to serve two very fundamental purposes. They would bear the weight of four enormous cables, and they would hold both the cables and the roadway of the bridge high enough so they would not interfere with traffic on the river.[13]

In similar fashion to the Brooklyn Bridge towers, rural America needs to rebuild with two "Economic Towers" necessary for the Adopt a Model™ program. The first tower is called the "Long Run Trend Tower" and the second the "Business Cycle Tower."

The Long Run Trend Tower

The *Long Run Trend Tower* concept emphasizes the general movement over time of particular measurement, especially one prone toward shorter-term fluctuations. One of the most important long-run trends in the study of macroeconomics is for real *gross domestic product* (GDP). The long-run trend of real GDP, which has historically increased about 3% a year, indicates the increase in the economy's production capabilities. Such capabilities have increased due to increases in the quantity and quality of resources. The total market value of all goods and services produced within the political boundaries of an economy during a given period of time is usually one year.[14]

The demands for a "Long Run Trend Tower" are essential for rural communities. America's growth was once based upon two factors: *colonization* and *industrialization.*

---

[13] http://www.nycroads.com/crossings/brooklyn/
[14] http://glossary.econguru.com/economic-term/GDP

Colonization occurs whenever any one or more species populate an area.[15] English colonization was essentially the beginning to all American expansion and industrialization. At the very beginning, the first settlers had the mindset to expand, to go beyond what had been inhabited before by anyone other than natives.

The moment the settlers landed, they were on a mission to build towns and harvest natural resources. The earliest forms of American industrialization and expansion started with the establishment of Jamestown, the first permanent English colony.

Not only did English colonization have an impact on the settlers, but it also greatly impacted the Native Americans who were on the land first and began to be pushed further and further off of their territory because of the growing need for American expansion. Along with the new colonies

---

[15] http://en.wikipedia.org/wiki/Colonization

came the Colombian Exchange, where not only people came back and forth from the old and new worlds, but so did animals, plants, resources, diseases, and many other different things. With different ideologies in mind, such as religious freedom or potential profits, the settlers flocked to America and established the beginnings of the era of expansion and *Industrialization*.[16]

The *Industrial Revolution* is one of the most far-reaching historical phenomena man has encountered. The technology advances in Europe not only resulted in the inventions of the printing press and the steam engine, it has also forged distinct changes in third world development.

Industrialization led to the quest for cheaper raw materials and labor to maximize profits. Industrialization led to a massive increase in demand for raw materials that could not be supported by local sources. Colonization was a natural byproduct of the need to control the source of additional material.

During the manufacturing age, industrialization swept across rural America. Companies sought cheaper land, cheaper labor and less regulation—the rural communities could accommodate these demands.

For the 21st Century, we are faced with new trends and developing challenges that shape the construction for a modern "Long Run Trend Tower." It begins with a knowledge-based society. There is a demand for communications and information technologies to offer rural areas

---

[16] http://www.xtimeline.com/evt/view.aspx?id=184440

the opportunity to overcome the traditional barriers of time and space, to attract high-paying, high technology, information-intensive jobs and to access information that could improve health care, education, and local governments. However, the technologies are not a cure-all. Rural economic development is a complex process that requires interaction among a multitude of players and institutions. Communications and information technologies can enhance and even make this process possible.

We are on the horizon of a new culture, which is being developed for this new "Long Run Trend,"—the *knowledge based society*. Two main variable ingredients always develop new cultures: Pleasure and Mobility.

Pleasure can be in the form of what makes you happy, what you may enjoy, or what entertainment is to you. Mobility could be planes, trains, and automobiles. This ingredient must be present in order for this new "Long Run Trend" to position you for future demand.

The form of pleasure in today's rural area may look like developed lakes, parks, fast internet for online activities and recreation. This attracts the family and virtual business demographics. Local business owners with remote control abilities in a metro region may want to raise their children in a more rural area, but that rural area must have specific capabilities to meet the demands of the family and businesses' needs.

Mobility today manifests through the transformation of knowledge, possibly in the form of WI-FI, cell phones, or electronics. However, the transformation of knowledge without wisdom creates a society of weak "yes men" and eventually a rebellious generation. American students are very independent and their parents disengaged. Graduate retention rates are at an all-time low in many small towns and are threatening the future of rural America. America's prominence in commerce, industry, science, and technological innovation is threatened by competition throughout the world.

Is it possible that even the responsibility to be a parent could be a vital principle to global sustainability? The strength of rural America has always been its morality and commitment to family, but it needs a few more ingredients to position itself for the future demand. We have to make the most of the communications and information technologies; a broad, holistic view of economic development is needed. Traditional economic development definitions, goals, and strategies have taken a one-dimensional approach, focusing on the business sector of a society or community and measuring development progress with standard economic indicators, not realizing the global impact.

The Business Cycle Tower

The second tower is the "Business Cycle Tower." A business cycle is the recurring, but irregular, pattern of business cycles, and its Macro view can be divided into two basic phases: *expansion* and *contraction*. An expansion is a period of increasing economic activity, and a contraction is a period of declining economic activity. These two phases are marked by two transitions. The transition from expan-

26

sion to contraction is termed a *peak,* and the transition from contraction to expansion is termed a *trough*. The early portion of an expansion is often referred to as a recovery.[17]

Assorted economic statistics that provide valuable information about the expansions and contractions of business cycles are grouped into three sets: lagging, coincident, and leading. Leading economic indicators tend to move up or down a few months BEFORE business-cycle expansions and contractions. Coincident economic indicators tend to reach their peaks and troughs at the same time as business cycles. Lagging economic indicators tend to rise or fall a few months after business-cycle expansions and contractions.[18]

Two factors are important when analyzing the "Business Cycle Tower;" they are the *booms* and the *busts*. A *boom* happens when there is a rise in production and credit expansions, and when agriculture and commodity prices increase. The cycle stops when a bust develops. A *bust* is caused when there is an over capacity of goods, debt compilation, and when monetary policies interfere with agriculture policies, which creates inflation and a loss of demand.

Two Tower Management System

In order to maintain in an economic downtrend, the "Two Tower Management System" must be implemented.

---

[17] http://glossary.econguru.com/economic-term/business+cycle +phases

[18] http://glossary.econguru.com/economic-term/business+cycle +indicators

Infrastructure is the key!

The "Long Run Trend Tower" needs to be managed by the Economic Development Board and the "Business Cycle Tower" managed by the Chamber of Commerce.

With current trends, a paradigm shift from industrialization to a knowledge-based society has transpired. A huge bust is occurring, and everyone is trying to figure out what to do next. Nevertheless, this new trend is going to create new booms. It is crucial for rural communities to position themselves to participate in the transition. Proper economic alignment is necessary to position one's self to develop strategic strategies to ride the storm as the trend passes into the next phase.

What Type of Bridge Do You Need?

With Adopt a Model™ system, SERE Administrative Services can assist you with a customized bridge for your community. It addresses the agricultural, manufacturing, education, business, cultural, and green issues that are relative to your specific need. This bridge is a partnership for rural America to the metro and global economy. With a holistic approach to economic development, you can maximize your existing resources, increase the quality of living, and develop long-range sustainability to a healthy and wealthy community.

CHAPTER TWO

Have A Blueprint

I N ORDER TO BUILD or assemble a bridge, a building, or a home, the success of its construction is centered on one main ingredient—a blueprint. A *blueprint* is a type of paper-based reproduction, usually of a technical drawing, documenting architecture or an engineering design. More generally, the term "blueprint" has come to be used to refer to any detailed plan.[19]

In this chapter, the correlation between a blueprint and the infrastructure of the Adopt a Model™ program will be illustrated to demonstrate the necessary and *detailed* "plan" used to build an economic base for growth in rural America. According to the U.S. Bureau of Labor Statistics, despite the construction sector's unemployment drop in April 2010, it continues to have by far the largest percentage of out-of-work Americans of any industry

---

[19] http://en.wikipedia.org/wiki/Blueprint

measured by BLS. So, if you are construction savvy, this section could be a light into the global economy.

Why a Blueprint?

Blueprints are much more detailed drawings than simple floor plans. Some people comprehend better with a 3D  image, stories, and simple illustrations, but some people would much rather have the blue print. This section caters more toward the blueprint readers, with detailed visuals and relative concepts in relation to the Adopt a Model™ program. Blueprints are exact detailed scaled drawings of plans of a home, building, or structure which include many more details than a basic floor plan.

Blueprint plans and specifications are the documents used by your builder and con-tractors to instruct them on how to build your new home. Each set of blueprints should include floor plans; plans for the foundation and information on footings and framing; front, side and rear elevations; roof plan; electrical layout; kitchen cabinet layout; and construction details.

These specified blueprints include detailed documentation which fully describe the quality and specifications of the materials needed to complete the building of a home.

Detailed blueprints can help get precise estimates of the total cost to build a new home, or in this case, a vibrant city.

Blueprints are used to provide the builder with a complete set of two-dimensional instructions on exactly how to construct the home. Likewise, the Adopt a Model™ system provides a series of two-dimensional plans to demonstrate and collaborate the necessary efforts to build a strong economy.

Specifications

Because the original drawings for the Brooklyn Bridge are protected by copyright, let us instead examine home construction designs as a metaphor, seeing how it is one of the largest industries impacted with unemployment.

When it comes to home construction, there are several necessary components to blueprints in order for the contractor to build the home. The size of the home and the needs of the occupants are reflected in the blueprints and exemplify the finished product according to the desires of the owner. Other than a basement, there are seven basic blueprint plans:

1. Floor Plans
2. Elevations
3. Electrical Layout
4. Framing Drawings
5. Plumbing and Mechanical Diagrams
6. Cross Section View
7. Plot Plan

Floor Plans

Let us examine each component of the home construction blueprint and see the comparison contrast to the Adopt a Model™ system, beginning with the first blueprint—*floor plans*. Floor plans are actually quite easy to understand. A floor plan layout on blueprints is basically an overhead view of the completed house. Dimensions are usually  drawn between the walls to specify room sizes and wall lengths. The floor plan locations of fixtures like sinks, water heaters, furnaces, etc. are easily recognizable.

Floor plans are drawn to scale so that if any specific dimension needed is missing, the contractor can scale the drawing to determine the right measurement. Any builder will know to look at the key provided on the house plan to determine the scale of the home. Since the blueprints are drawn to scale, if any portion needs to be changed, the contractor can scale the drawing to determine the right measurements to make the adjustments.

A Chamber Meeting for Workforce Development

Floor plans for the development of a prosperous rural community can be described with the following goals.

These objects include:

a. The availability of useful and satisfying work for community members, with a new workforce development program;

b. Access to biological and social resources and necessities;

c. A thriving, vital local economy;[20]

d. Improved rural income levels and employment opportunities;

e. Improved access by rural residents to adequate housing and essential community facilities and services; and

f. Responsible use of rural resources and the rural environment to preserve the rural quality of life.[21]

g. Business and graduate retention rate improvement and future careers visible and obtainable.

---

[20] Thomas Power, *The Economic Pursuit of Quality* (Armonk, NY: M.E. Sharpe, Inc., 1998), footnote 6, pp. 169-174.

[21] Kenneth Deavers, "Social Science contributions to Rural Development Policy in the 1980's," *American Journal of Agricultural Economics* 62(5), pp. 10-21.

Together, these sets of goals provide the development of a rural environment that supports the well-being and health of people, as well as the businesses they support, work at, and/or manage. By addressing both the human and business conditions in a community, the floor plans emphasize the fundamental linkages between these two aspects of community life.

Elevations

Second, *elevation* blueprints generally include four drawings of a home: the front, the rear, and each side. The purposes of these drawings, which are drawn to scale, are so measurements can be taken for any necessary aspect and also to indicate what the home will look like upon completion. Elevations are a non-perspective view of the home.

Elevation plans illustrate the vertical elements within your landscape design and describe all of the details needed to build these features. Most of the time, an elevation plan does *not* represent the entire structure. Instead, a side portion of the landscape element is drawn, showing the construction details that are used throughout the structure.

This particular type of landscape design plan may include a variety of different features and is often integrated into the concept design plan. Fencing, pool areas, walls, outdoor kitchens, and many other elements may be illustrated with landscape design elevation plans. Elevation blueprints also include ridge heights, exterior finishes, roof pitches, and other design aspects to give a general idea of the finished home. These exterior specifications can also provide details about the home's exterior architectural styling.[22]

An *economic elevation plan* is the visual perception for the long-range goals and objectives, typically like a financial plan, which establishes the strategic provisions and stability for employment, income, expansion and growth the development in a rural community needs. Similar to a home construction elevation plan, a financial elevation plan demonstrates the finished product from four points of view:

1. Employment
2. Income and Revenue
3. Health and Social Benefits
4. Stability

View #1: The availability of employment opportunities provides jobs that are useful and satisfying.

This view must incorporate the quality of employment, opportunity for advancement, and income levels associated with such employment, both to individuals and to the community. When it comes to creating more jobs, the need

---

[22] http://www.landscape-design-advisor.com/landscape-design-elevation-plans.html

must meet the demand. Too often, financial consultants fail to recognize that imported jobs often attract imported labor. This being said, even when indigenous workers become employed, they might remain poorly paid or under-employed due to greater competition with imported labor.

Job training is important to overcoming the obstacle of a poorly or inappropriately skilled local labor-force. Many Federal training efforts in this arena are administered by the Department of Labor. Vocational education, work experience programs, and cooperative extension reinforce human resource training are provided by United Support™.

With the Adopt a Model™ system, SAS can assist rural communities in economic development that will produce hundreds and thousands of jobs through its myriad of resources such as agriculture, a strategic business eco-system, green technology, education, new innovative workforce development programs, and much more.

View #2: The job development provides income levels consistent with the financial needs of the region.

Jobs must provide adequate income for workers. More than 70 percent of the poor in non-metro areas work full or part-time jobs during the year.[23] For a variety of reasons, jobs in rural areas often do not pay enough for workers to emerge from poverty. Among the year-round, part-time workers in rural areas, 39 percent are under-employed. Many work

---

[23] Center on Budget and Policy Priorities, *Laboring for Less: Working but Poor in Rural America* (Washington, DC: 1990), p. 7

part-time, not because they prefer to, but because it is the only available employment.[24]

Adopt a Model™ assists communities to growth, development and expansion, using natural resources and by connecting the community with other regions in the U.S. and overseas who have a demand for their services and goods.

View #3: A holistic approach provides access for community members to necessities such as health services and adequate housing, as well as to social necessities, such as government services and educational opportunities.

The health and social welfare of the people are essential elements to a community's economic and overall well-

---

[24] J.F. Coates, Inc., "Work in Rural America," contractor report prepared for the Office of Technology Assessment, 1990, p. 22.

being. Though more difficult to identify, social necessities are indispensable to a community's well-being.

The SAS Adopt a Model™ provides the necessary resources for training and for consultation to development government services and education. Education is the fundamental component to gain useful and satisfying work which devises solutions to problems and the ability to adapt to change, qualities that are integral to maintaining community welfare.

View #4: The local participation and process for sustain-able development provides stability and a self-contained, vital community.

Stability and a sense of local control go hand and hand as critical ingredients for establishing an environment where people and enterprises can flourish. Local control vests decisions and planning for the community's future with those who stand to benefit. Because development has been done *to* rural communities rather than *by* them, the fruits of rural development have not accrued to rural citizens.

Unlike some rural development programs that design their program to capture the benefits of outside firms and neglect the development of local resources, Adopt a Model™ designs a strategy for sustainable development that avoids the dependency upon a single firm, industry, or outside government agency. Instead, we find alternatives in which the community participates as equals, rather than pawns in the development game.

Electrical Layout

Third, in home construction there is the *electrical layout*. Electrical diagrams (if provided) can often be difficult to read, which is why the drawings of the electrical layout of a home are often on a separate drawing. By keeping the electrical layout on its own drawing, the electrician can begin wiring the home without reading through the entire building floor plan.

The layout will show locations of light fixtures, fans, outlets, light switches, etc. There is usually a legend on the page, which explains what each symbols represents. For illustration purposes, a legend chart is often necessary for a novice to understand the symbols.

ELECTRICAL SYMBOL LEGEND

STANDARD LIGHT	TELEPHONE JACK
STANDARD SWITCH	THERMOSTAT
3-WAY SWITCH	DOORBELL
FAN LIGHT	SMOKE DETECTOR
REC. FAN	STANDARD OUTLET
CHANDELIER	GFCI OUTLET
BREAKER PANEL	220 OUTLET
CABLE HOOK-UP	CEILING OUTLET

The *economic* electrical layout is the power source for business development—"How you start is how you will finish." The high-tech communication systems interface the other components that need energy for sustainability. This area is often confusing to some because they are not trained to read the *"legends."* So let me help here. Would you agree that our local small businesses are not empowered enough to be sustained for future demand? Would you agree that maybe something is hindering growth and success for our small businesses?

A great error in today's entrepreneurial trend is the owner-operated business model. This model's intent was for ma and pa shops, not entrepreneurs. The old cliché "small business is the backbone to this nation" resembles a disjointed spine with a 90% failure rate in small businesses. This huge unsuccessful backbone contributes at least 60%

to the divorce rates tearing apart the true backbone of our nation—the family. We have less than 7% of the small business industry educated enough to make an impact. The opposite of impact is "no work."

To assure a more viable future for this country, the owner-operated business model should be replaced with the accurate business models available. If you have an owner-operated business, then this is what you have: you built the business to depend on you, and unless you are bionic, it will burn you out. Your accountant will then depreciate the business to no capital value; your spouse is almost done with you; the kids need you, and you do not know how to get out of the business or transition to success. If this does not describe you, then I am proud of you and you are a minority. Congratulations.

SAS has built a business ecosystem that supports the small business and provides strategic financial services to help sustain you in order for you to obtain the very reason you started a company—to build a legacy for your family. I started designing this ecosystem in 2006 because I found myself losing grips with my wife and children—chasing the dream but only really maintaining a delusion of a business. I designed the system for myself, but I realized through consulting businesses that it really was to help others. I now see it as a family preservation tool for all business owners. The economic electrical layout is the power source for business development. It should support the businesses in sustainability and position them for future demand.

Framing Drawings

Like every other drawing in the home-building plan, the framing drawings (if provided) are also drawn to scale. Framing plans include the basic skeletal structure of the home. Floor joist locations, walls, and roof trusses are the overall detail of these plans.

In an *economic framing drawing*, the structural components show the framework for building a successful infrastructure between the rural community and the necessary outside agencies, which combine and hold the Adopt a Model™ system together. It includes specific industrial solutions for the educational, business, environmental, socio economics, financial, and tax credits that position each *rural* area for future demand.

Each industry and every moving part in that industry affects the local and global economy. Some would beg to differ, but we no longer have that boundary as a national economy anymore. At one time, international trade depended on *rural* America, but not anymore. Instead, offshore outsourcing and cheaper import solutions have distracted this nation from its roots. Now, each locality has a responsibility to be educated on macroeconomics from a holistic and global view to stay competitive and sustained.

The Adopt a Model™ program is a vehicle for combining the strengths, abilities, and hopes of a community for future health and wealth.

Plumbing and Mechanical Diagrams

Fifth, is the *Plumbing and Mechanical Diagrams*. These systems are generally not covered extensively on the blueprints other than locations of fixtures and main service lines. If you are going through the expense of a more complicated heating system like in-floor radiant heat or even an engineered forced air system, these drawings need to be completed by a heating or plumbing specialist. This information is ample for the contractor to install a plumbing system.

The *economic plumbing and mechanical diagrams* provide the necessary facility services. Just as water is necessary for a home, having the proper facilities is equally important. Adopt a Model™ can assist with fluidity as well as waste removal. The Adopt a Model™ program is a cooperative business model with an additive integration that reduces price points, eliminates waste, and sustains the business cycle.

In addition, SAS can provide the necessary strategic provisions and planning to position a rural area for future demands and growth.

Cross Section View

Sixth, the *Cross Section View* provides overhead views, or floor plan views of the structure, with detailed information about wall lengths and room dimensions, but do not fully provide enough information for successful construction of the home. A cross section of a home is a drawing of the completed home as if it were sliced in half. This part of a home plan provides the builder with an even better understanding of the relativity of floor heights and rafter lengths, among other structural elements of the home. Therefore, in most cases, a cross section of the home is included in a set of house plans.

An *economic cross section* view is the business overview providing a scale of options in the financial venture. It allows the participants a better relativity of the financial heights, lengths and other structure elements for business loans, grants and matching fund programs. In other words, the *economic cross view* enables you to understand where you're headed with your socioeconomic development. Where do you want your rural city or community to be in three to five years? How do you achieve your goals and objectives based upon the current economic trends and environment developments? What are your limitations?

The SAS Adopt a Model™ provides financial solutions such as free business consulting, merchant cash advances, unsecured business credits, SBA loans, 401k rollover options, equipment financing, and assistance with accounts receivables and purchase orders. The following chapters will address this cross section view in detail to educate and encourage hope for an economy in financial crisis.

Plot Plan

Seventh, *Plot Plans* are comprehensive drawings of the site location or lot on which a new home is to be built. Plot plans are drawn to determine the placement of the home on the chosen building lot in reference to the property boundaries, topography, and house layout. Plot dimensions are normally recorded by a surveyor and are used to determine the exact location and positioning of the selected home in relationship to the chosen lot. Plot plans will typically include the location of utility services, set back requirements, easements, locations of driveways and walkways. In some cases, a topographical map may be included that will supply the architect or builder with critical data on the slope and terrain of the lot he or she is designing a home for.

The *economic plot plan* for the Adopt a Model™ program is a business ecosystem. A business ecosystem is defined as "an economic community supported by a foundation of interacting organizations and individuals—the organisms of the business world." This economic community produces goods and services of value to customers, who are themselves members of the ecosystem. The member organizations also include suppliers, lead producers, competitors, and other stakeholders.

Over time, they co-evolve their capabilities and roles and tend to align themselves with the directions set by one or more central companies. Those companies holding leadership roles may change over time, but the function of the ecosystem leader is valued by the community because it enables members to move toward shared visions to align their investments and to find mutually supportive roles."[25]

The business economic system suggests that a business environment is established when a cohesive effort with other companies is present, and that "the particular niche a business occupies is challenged by newly arriving species."[26] This means that companies need to become proactive in developing mutually beneficial relationships with customers, suppliers, and even competitors.

Bio-ecosystem is the study of the reciprocal relationship between business and organisms and their environments. The goal of this "business ecology" is sustainability with the business solutions when companies work together on strategy, design, and project management.

The same can be said for industries and manufacturers, such as the motor vehicle factories. Ford Motors did well using methods of mass production, assembly line, and insourcing. This is why the ASP (application service provider) industry moved forward. It combines a working relationship of networks and focuses upon the core competencies. According to the gospel of Cisco Systems, companies who are inclined to exist together within an

---

[25] James F. Moore, *The Death of Competition: Leadership and Strategy in the Age of Business Ecosystems*, (New York: Harper Business, 1996), p. 26.

[26] Moore, p. 3.

"ecosystem" facilitate the imminence of Internet-based application delivery.[27]

The ecosystem concept was widely used by Cisco Systems Inc. throughout the world. The company leveraged partners for all business functions except for developing their core patented products and business strategy. Partners were used for sales, marketing, manufacturing, technical support, and new installations. Cisco lived up to the motto, "Do what you do best and leave the rest for others to do."[28]

Reading a Blueprint

Here's the bottom line: not everyone can read a blueprint. Architectural drawings are not for the novice; they are for the professionally skilled laborer that specializes in a specific field in construction. Without a blueprint, the project cannot succeed; the success of a home or building depends upon it.

Rural communities are struggling to find answers for the economic crisis in their region. They need an *eco-blueprint*!

A person's skills, education, experience, and business knowledge will determine which of the seven blueprints are easier to understand. For some, they will only grasp the floor plan or plot plan. For others, they will comprehend the more technical blueprints, such as the electrical or plumbing diagrams.

---

[27] Ilene Kaminsky, "ASPs – Creating a New business Ecology", June 5, 2002, paragraph 1.

[28] http://en.wikipedia.org/wiki/Business_ecosystem

The same can be said when it comes to the Adopt a Model™ system. It is intended to be an *eco-blueprint* assisting rural America with viable solutions to a struggling economy. However, when a board or a committee from a city or county analyze the Adopt a Model™ *eco-blueprint*, not everyone will understand or grasp the enormity of its proposal. It will take a team effort from each participant to trust those who have the skill, knowledge, or experience to grasp the concepts explained.

The *eco-blueprint* may seem overwhelming or intimidating, but without it, struggling communities will continue to die. SAS can prevent some funerals!

CHAPTER THREE

Invest in People

TODAY'S AVERAGE AMERICAN finds themselves overwhelmed and anxious in a world of economic and political uncertainty. With a bubble burst from a collapsed economy, corporate banks that are going bankrupt, a mortgage meltdown, a housing crash, Wall Street bailouts, high unemployment, the death of the auto industry, a deflated dollar, and rising gas prices, it has caused many to wonder where our nation is headed. It appears that history is repeating itself. What's the answer?

History of the Workforce Development Program

The concept of a *workforce development* has a long history with Democrats and Republicans, private sectors, and not-for-profit organizations, which have attempted to provide job assistance in rural America during difficult times of economic hardship. In 1933, the *Works Progress Administration* was part of the *New Deal* established by President Franklin D. Roosevelt to combat the challenges of the Great Depression. In 1939, the *Works Progress Administration* was renamed as the *Works Project Administration* and it was the largest and most ambitious New Deal agency, employing millions of unskilled workers to carry out public works projects, including the construction of public buildings and roads. It also operated large arts, drama, media, and literacy projects. It fed children and redistributed food, clothing, and housing. Almost every community in the United States had a park, bridge, or school constructed by the agency, which especially benefited rural and Western areas.

In 1973, the *Comprehensive Employment and Training Act* (CETA) was passed into law to train workers and provide jobs to those with low incomes and long term unemployment. This training was provided by public agencies and private not-for-profit organizations.

In 1982, the *Job Training Partnership Act* (JTPA) passed into law under the Regan administration and was ratified to establish federal assistance programs to prepare youth (ages 14-21) and un-skilled adults for entry into the labor force, and to provide job training to economically disadvantaged and other individuals facing serious barriers to employment. A formula established for distribution of funds to the states caused political turmoil.

In 1985, studies showed that the formulas were affected by a state's political power to influence the votes of representatives, which brought into question the distribution of funds. Researchers investigating found that certain regions, such as the upper Midwest, were over-funded, while other regions, such as the South, were underfunded.[29]

In 1998, during the Clinton administration, politicians demonstrated a mounting interest in growing trends with progressive workforce development concepts and implemented the American *Workforce Investment Act* (WIA).  Enacted during Bill Clinton's second term, it represented an attempt to induce businesses to participate in the local delivery of Workforce Development Services. The principal vehicle for this was *Workforce Investment Boards* (WIBs) that worked with federal, state, and local funding to implement workforce development programs. Every community in the fifty states (and province of the US) is

---

[29] *Race and Sex Discrimination in the Operation of the Job Training Partnership Act.* July 17, 1991. Congressional Sales office.

associated with a Local WIB (LWIB). For each LWIB, a chief elected official (i.e., county commissioner or a mayor of a lead city) appoints members to sit on the WIB. At least 50% of their board members must be from the private sector.

WIBs work in conjunction with economic development related organizations in order to maximize the reaction time and create resources to intervene for both the dislocated workforce and the incumbent workforce members of a community. One of those economic development organizations is Sere Administrative Services (SAS).

Sere Administrative Services (SAS) is a privately operated non-profit organization and a resourceful workforce development agency whose main role is to work collectively with private businesses, financial sponsors, and non-profit, federal, state and local agencies, providing funding, education and training, career development, and back office management services that offer sustainable and innovative solutions for economic growth and job expansion.

Unfortunately, the signs of a global economic downturn hit in 2008. The danger of a global economic crisis can spread across the globe and drastically collapse a nation overnight. Many financial and economic experts agree that the global economy has experienced the worst recession since the Great Depression of the 1930s. Again, history appears to be repeating itself.

Current Trends

The U.S. financial crisis had at its core the subprime housing market. Home loans were made to unqualified buyers in violation of prudent lending practices as well as lending regulations. The banks making the loans did not hold on to them. Instead, they sold them to secondary mortgage consolidators, who then packaged them into derivative financial instruments. These, in turn, were sold to investors across the globe, who suffered severe losses when the loans went into default. There followed a major credit crisis and many banks and investing houses failed. This created a domino effect in the economy.

Without access to credit due to bank failures and an overall decline in the lenders' abilities to provide credit even to financially sound businesses and individuals, consumer spending has severely declined. In particular, the businesses selling big-ticket items, such as the auto industry, have been especially hit hard. Further, a large proportion of the goods sold in stores within the United States are imported. Therefore, countries around the world are experiencing the backlash of the U.S. economic crisis with associated declines in foreign trade, number of firms and employment. As U.S. companies export their job services to other nations, U.S. local economies experience plant closings on an accelerating scale.

Workforce Development in Action

Workforce development is an American economic development approach that attempts to improve a region's economic stability and prosperity, a human resources strategy focusing on people rather than businesses. Workforce development has evolved from a problem-focused approach, addressing issues such as low-skilled workers or the need for more employees in a particular industry, to a holistic approach considering participants many barriers and the overall needs of the region. SAS workforce development programs focus on solutions to social equity issues.

SAS has two workforce development strategies: *place-based* strategies that attempt to address the needs of people living in a particular neighborhood, and *sector-based* strategies that focus on matching workers' skills to needs in an industry already present in the region, such as healthcare or manufacturing. Some contemporary workforce development programs attempt to combine elements of both approaches, linking employment training with other government programs and community resources to provide wraparound services.

Across both approaches, themes for best practices have emerged. The SAS workforce development programs have a strong network of ties in the community and are equipped to respond to changes in their environments. Additionally, SAS takes a holistic approach to the problems faced by participants. The effectiveness of these programs has been evaluated in various ways, including quantitative and qualitative techniques. Ideally, random assignment methods are used, although their utilization may be difficult in practice.

The responsibility for workforce development in the United States has rested on the government's shoulders for at least a century—since the advent of public schools.[30] This formal system of education replaced earlier days in American history when students whose parents desired them to learn a trade other than their parents' were apprenticed. Informal schooling took place at home, depending on the household's ability and income level. Public schools were created to prepare students to earn a living wage by providing them with skills such as reading and arithmetic. However, an employer still typically provided vocational training on the job.

Traditional workforce development has been problem-focused. Economic development practitioners evaluated neighborhoods, cities, or states on the basis of perceived

---

[30] Blakely, Edward; Leigh, Nancy Green, *Planning Local Economic Development,* (Thousand Oaks, CA: Sage Publications Inc., 2010)

weaknesses in human resource capacity. However, recent efforts view workforce development in a more positive light. Economic developers use workforce development as a way to increase equity among inhabitants of a region. Inner-city residents may not have access to equal education opportunities, and workforce development programs can increase their skill level so they can compete with suburbanites for high-paying jobs.

The SAS workforce development through Adopt a Model™ has also expanded beyond the notion of employment or vocational training. Workforce development today often takes a more holistic approach, addressing issues such as spatial mismatch or poor transportation to jobs. Programs to train workers are often part of a network of other human service or community opportunities.

These types of partnerships allow SAS to develop workforce development programs and employ change. In the 1990s, sector-based workforce development programs were most commonly found in nonprofit, community-based organizations, but today they are more likely to be tied to community colleges. Additionally, sector-based programs are now more likely to be paid for by government funding rather than private donations.

Our Approach

SAS takes two approaches to workforce development, *sector-based* and *place-based*. The sectoral advocate speaks for the demand side, emphasizing employer or market-driven strategies, whereas the place-based practitioner is resolutely a believer in the virtue of the supply side: those low-income job seekers who need work and a pathway out of poverty. However, SAS believes the best approach is a mixed approach.

SAS approaches the sectors, or industries, in a region that is in need of specific workplace skills. These strategies focus on the demand side of workplace development and consider the industries in which it is most likely that new employees will be hired. Providing the right program is crucial. Sector-based programs have higher entrance requirements than place-based strategies because their ultimate aim is to aid the sector at which they are targeted, not to increase the general hirability of the most disadvantaged residents.

The Adopt a Model™ approach focuses primarily upon people and not profit. This is not to say SAS is not interested in monetary results, but rather speaks to its philosophy, which is—if you invest in people, growth will follow. Human capital is more valuable than money! SAS believes in a social-driven society. A society that creates hope, innovates answers, and inspires dreams. A system that starts with today's youth, age 14, learning skills that will open doors to public service and capitalism. A system that helps local schools create internships and educational programs.

For too long, workforce development programs have failed because their focus is on building big businesses and not investing in people. What makes SAS different is its vision. It is a vision that demonstrates a genuine compassion, caring for people, and it is a team who does what they do because they believe people matter most. It is just as important to build self-esteem, self-confidence, and self-worth as it is to find an adequate job. Investing in others creates a competitive environment and at the same time establishes unity.

SAS helps people restore their credit, obtain transportation, make a living, possess their own vehicle, find reasonable health care, child care, and resources for child development. In addition, SAS believes that a business society builds people by providing strong education programs in the fields, that based upon economic and cultural factors, are always hiring. Focusing on a socioeconomic growth pattern empowers the people of a community to want to reinvest back into their community. People who own and finance co-ops use it. If they own and invest in the city where they live, they will contribute and benefit from that city. They gain a sense of pride and are the ones who take responsibility for the city. A holistic approach combined with a strong business cycle produces a rich community.

Sector Based Strategies

SAS implements sector-based strategies that are designed to fit the needs of both industry employers and workers who want to improve their skills and advance their career development. By definition, sector-based approaches target a definite business type. An initial assessment can reveal which industries would be good targets for a rural community, and assessments during the program can help refine the program's focus.

With the SAS Adopt a Model™ strategies, relationships are typically created through networks and partnerships (between invested employers, unions, Workforce Investment Boards, centers, adult basic education providers, community based organizations, com-munity colleges and other institutions of higher education, or other training and service providers). These partnerships are designed to connect SAS with low-income or disadvant-aged individuals with employment in jobs that offer the promise of financial stability and significant growth in the industry in the near future.

Community involvement is also an important component in building a sector-based strategy. Specifically, the involve-ment of an intermediary with deep knowledge of the industry is necessary. The intermediary can facilitate partnerships with employers, and help create solutions for both employers and potential employees. SAS encourages employers to participate in activities such as developing curriculum, creating evaluation and assessment tools, and committing to job shadow programs.

Because the sector approach targets an entire sector, rather than a single company, SAS involves the government and capital ventures to work side-by-side with industry leaders to help an entire sector become more competitive. Through such strategies for improving the employability and career path development for low-income, low-skilled workers, SAS believes an Adopt a Model™ strategy benefits both employers and workers. Some government grants require a percentage of funding to come from private sources, which ensures that the community and targeted industry are invested in the program before it starts. Because public sector financial support is often small, SAS can leverage private sector investments by increasing awareness to potential investors and private companies who are seeking the "right" community in which to invest.

Obstacles

Several potential barriers exist for employing sector-based workforce development strategies. First, in many regions a skills gap exists between what workers know and what employers need. Although demand might be high for a particular occupation, it may be unrealistic to train a low-skill population in the necessary skills. Second, rapid change makes sector-based strategies difficult. Quick turnover in technology can make a training program obsolete in a few years.

Last, many potential workers in the United States demonstrate low literacy or educational levels. In some regions, the SAS workforce development programs will have to teach basic skills like reading as well as giving instruction in tasks that are more specialized. With the rise of immigration, language barriers prevent individuals from obtaining a job. If a community has language and literacy barriers, they will not qualify for skilled jobs. This not only hurts the individuals, but it also hurts the region from obtaining interest from industries that are looking for a community to which they will build a manufacturing plant.

Placed Based Strategies

SAS also uses *place-based* approaches, which consider the supply side of the workplace (workers), and are primarily focused on the characteristics of PEOPLE in the region or community where the training program will be located. Using this system, SAS helps participants gain initial access to the labor market while addressing other essential concerns to the region, such as housing development or

English skills. In general, SAS targets training the unemployed workers and enhancing their skills for entering the labor market.

Some have been quick to criticize place-based strategies for their focus on finding jobs for participants quickly, rather than evaluating the quality of those jobs. However, SAS approaches have provided an ideal framework for state and local government to address the issue of unemployment and poverty problems in local communities or regions. SAS strongly believes that a place-based effort will focus on the most pressing needs of local residents, such as physical or substance abuse or financial difficulties, along with providing employment training. The program we employ will provide mentors who can connect participants to resources, rather than undertaking the large financial burden of providing these services. Some approaches now combine a focus on place, with an evaluation of sectors that face a workforce or skill shortage.

Pre-assessment of Community Needs

Prior to implementing a sector or place-based approach, SAS conducts an analysis of the community's current and anticipated needs. When SAS evaluates the community, a sector analysis can determine the need for more healthcare workers in a particular community, or assess whether employees' salaries increased because of the program. A SAS analysis also considers whether the participants were employed at a higher rate than prior to participating in the program. Another common indication is retention, or whether employees stay employed, although this data, in most cases, can be difficult to collect.

Employer Resourcing

The SAS Adopt a Model™ system employs both sector and place-based strategies that can emphasize the importance of ties with the employers. Even in place-based strategies focused on finding work quickly, it must tie efforts to employers to determine who is hiring. These relationships should occur before the program is implemented to help shape a curriculum that responds to the employers' needs.

SAS also provides programs that not only determine the general skills that are lacking in a specific population, such as English-speaking skills, but also provides literacy and language programs for those in need. The SAS workforce development programs can evaluate what is needed based on the strength and number of ties with community employers during the creation stage of the program, as well as their ongoing participation to assess which skills are most needed.

Community Resourcing

SAS believes place and sector based programs benefit from a strong network of ties to community non-profits and other resources. Many Adopt a Model™ programs can work with community colleges to provide the needed support, but any "base in a strong community organization" is beneficial for a successful workforce development program. Because SAS is a not-for-profit and private entity, one of its strong efforts is to work with non-profit organizations, because studies show they have been found to be essential for successful sector-based programs, despite the programs' inherent focus on industry and employers.

Financial Assistance

An adverse financial situation can be a huge detriment to participants in the workforce development program. SAS has a variety of ways to address these needs, but the important aspect is that financial difficulties in particular are not ignored. Providing financial assistance to individualized services such as childcare or help in over-coming substance abuse is also an important component of the SAS workforce development.

A strong workforce development program will provide assistance in the areas most needed by program participants, most notably, financial assistance. This does not necessarily mean the program provides finances; SAS works directly with program's mentors who help workers find government or non-profit sources.

Adaptability

Not every program works in every area. Flexibility is a key, so that programs can change when market or workforce conditions change. One marker of adaptability is the presence of mechanisms to listen to what the community is saying, evidenced by the close ties with community stakeholders and non-profits as explained above. SAS has working relationships with local Chambers of Commerce and community action organizations to keep communication strong and implement the strategies in that local community. However, some difficulties may arise due to organizational culture. Once the issue is identified, a solution is implemented to understand what the breakdown is and how to fix it.

Adaptability is closely tied to scale and sustainability. SAS has successful programs to update their goals on an ongoing basis in order to respond and strengthen information systems that relay the current situation of the job market and employers' needs.

Organizational capacity

One of the concerns that SAS addresses is with a program's human resources (or staff size) and funding. Successful organizations possess the capacity for implementing large scale programs deeply invested in the community's culture and needs. Although programs do not always provide internal support mechanisms such as childcare, they should have adequate organizational capacity to assist participants in finding the type of support they need. Furthermore, maintaining current, constant communication with

employers and with non-profits, as well as other community organizations, requires significant staff time. SAS
provides successful programs that are prepared for the work
it takes to implement a workforce development program.

Cost-benefit Analysis

SAS performs a cost-benefit analysis, comparing the costs
of implementing a program to the benefits accrued to
stakeholders. A cost-benefit analysis can demonstrate
whether a program saves money due to lower welfare or
social service needs, and whether a program will raise the
average earnings of participants. Even if a program results
in net costs to the grantor or investor, if every dollar spent
results in more than a dollar earned by program
participants, long-run trends show whether it is a worth-
while endeavor.

SAS also performs a cost benefit analysis because some
benefits and costs cannot be expressed in dollars. For
example, the emotional stability that results from the

security of a job is difficult to quantify. Although methods exist for monetizing factors like these, some evaluators choose instead to focus only on factors that can be reliably measured.

Evaluation

Researchers have used multiple methods to determine whether workforce development programs are successful. Generally, researchers want answers to questions such as whether programs result in higher employment among participants, whether employment is long-term, and whether participants make higher wages than before they entered the program. Some methods are qualitative and some are quantitative.

SAS uses the Adopt a Model™ system, which works with the two primary resources to guarantee success: (1) The Long-Run Trend and (2) The Business Cycle model. By combining these two, the results speak for themselves. As the Adopt a Model™ program goes forth, the back office support tracks the progress and can give internal evaluates to its co-ops. SAS has the software solutions to track efforts to outcomes where it pertains to workforce development.

CHAPTER FOUR

A Band-Aid Won't Work

THE SMALL TOWNS that make up what is known as rural America have taken a hard economic hit. In fact, there have been reports over the years of rural America dying.

Yet, a new report released recently by the Carsey Institute at the University of New Hampshire (UNH) brings to mind that famous quote from Mark Twain: "The reports of my death are greatly exaggerated." Not because white farming families, who had left their farms in search of city employment, are returning, but because young Latino families are now calling rural America home—"young" being the operative word.

In the report, Rural Demographic Change in the New Century: Slower Growth, Increased Diversity, the authors found that while the rural population growth slowed because fewer people were moving into rural areas after 2000, diversity actually accelerated. Racial and ethnic minorities accounted for 83 percent of rural growth between 2000-2010. Researchers say Latinos are to be credited for most of that growth.[31]

Kenneth Johnson, senior demographer at the Carsey Institute and professor of sociology at UNH, pointed out that though minorities accounted for the majority of rural population gain between 2000 and 2010, minorities still only represent just 21 percent of the rural population overall. Johnson, who analyzed the census numbers, said common threads among the dying counties are older whites, who are no longer having children, and an exodus of young adults, who find little promise in the region and seek jobs elsewhere. The places also have fewer Hispanic

---

[31] http://www.carseyinstitute.unh.edu/publications/IB-Johnson-Rural-Demographic-Trends.pdf

immigrants, who on average are younger and tend to have more children than other groups.[32]

"The downturn in the U.S. economy is only exacerbating the problem," said Johnson, whose research paper was published in the journal Rural Sociology. "In some cases, the only thing that can pull an area out is an influx of young Hispanic immigrants or new economic development." Yet, what makes this discovery promising is the children in Latino families who are settling in rural America.

In all, roughly 760 of the nation's 3,142 counties are fading away, stretching from industrial areas near Pittsburgh and Cleveland to the vineyards outside San Francisco to the rural areas of east Texas and the Great Plains. Once-booming housing areas, such as retirement communities in Florida, have not been immune.

West Virginia was the first to experience natural decrease statewide over the last decade, with Maine, Pennsylvania, and Vermont close to following suit, according to the latest census figures. As a nation, the U.S. population grew by just 9.7 percent since 2000, the lowest decennial rate since the Great Depression.[33]

Dying counties in the U.S. were rare until the 1960s, when the baby boom ended. By 1973, as farming communities declined, roughly 515 counties—mostly in the Great

---

[32]

http://www.ksagland.com/index.php?option=com_content&view=articl e &id=4817:census-estimates-show-1-in-4-us-counties-are-dying &catid=36: national-ag-news&Itemid=84

[33] http://www.census.gov

Plains—reported natural decrease. The phenomenon then began to show up in industrial regions, such as upstate New York and California. Natural decrease peaked in 2002 at a record 985, or 1 in 3 counties, before increasing births and an influx of Hispanic immigration helped add to county populations during the housing boom.

Following the recent recession, birth rates have dropped to the lowest in a century. Preliminary census numbers for 2007-09 now show that the number of dying counties is back on the upswing. Recent additions include Pittsburgh and its surrounding counties.

James Follain, senior fellow and economist at the Nelson A. Rockefeller Institute of Government at the University of Albany, said a new kind of declining city may be emerging in the wake of the housing bust—metropolitan areas that rapidly overbuilt earlier in the decade and then suffered massive foreclosures.

He cited as examples Las Vegas, Miami, parts of Arizona, and Stockton, Modesto, Fresno, and Riverside in California. Like traditional ghost towns, Follain says, portions of these areas could spiral down from persistent loss of jobs and population and lose their reason for being.

Follain also pointed to a tighter fiscal environment in Washington that will limit help to troubled areas.[34] House

---

[34] http://www.nytimes.com/2011/02/16/us/politics/16congress.html

Republicans also are pushing federal spending cuts of more than $61 billion, even if it means reducing jobs.[35]

"It's going to be a very slow recovery," Follain said.

Rural America is dying out. You may have heard that, but our latest census count backs it up. Reporter Hope Yen has done a series of articles for the Associated Press about the 2010 census and the trends we're seeing. Here's one trend: Rural places hold only 16 percent of the nation's population. That's the lowest ever. It was 20 percent in the year 2,000. It was 72 percent a hundred years ago. [36]

Central cities are still doing okay. Their population grew by 3 percent, compared to the 2,000 census. But the big winners were (you guessed it) the suburbs, which now hold more than half of the American population. The growth and expansion of suburbs has created the American megalopolis. That's being manifested in the merger of cities like Tampa and Orlando, Austin and San Antonio… maybe even Phoenix and Tucson.

Births have always exceeded deaths in the United States by a substantial margin, so little attention has been paid to specific areas where more people die than are born. Yet, in some parts of rural America, deaths have exceeded births for decades.

---

[35] http://alfin2100.blogspot.com/2011/02/dying-us-counties-baby-bust-phenomenon.html

[36] http://www.kpbs.org/news/2011/aug/01/rural-decline-and-endless-city/

The ebbs and flows of natural decrease over the last half century have gone largely unnoticed. Yet the pronounced spatial clustering of natural decrease coupled with its protracted incidence in some rural areas underscores the significant implication it has for the future of these regions. With few young adults and a growing older population, the future viability of many natural decrease areas is not encouraging.

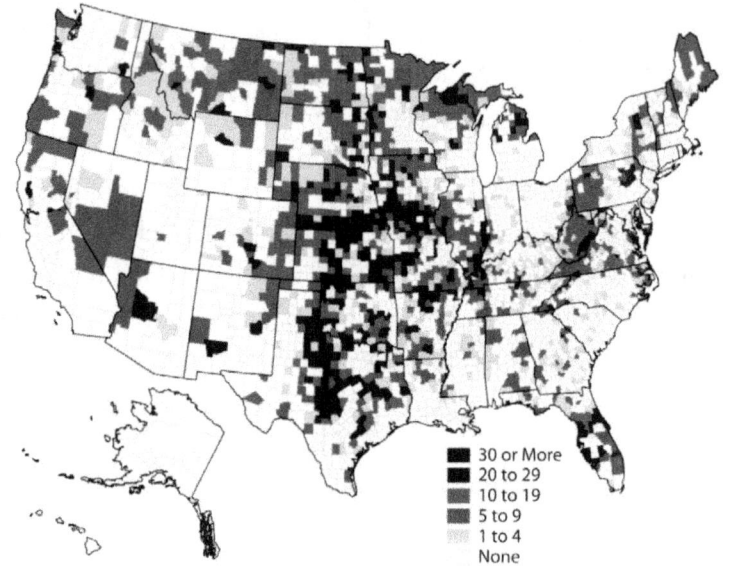

Carsey Institute. Data from Census Bureau and National Center for Health Statistics.

As the nation faces the 1990s, farmers and small-town citizens no longer live in the countryside found in a Willa Cather novel or on a Norman Rockwell canvas. Today there are two rural Americas: one dying, the other surviving—often by its wits.

Isolated, one-industry towns and back-road hamlets that once defined "country" are fading into history. At the same time modern little communities with diverse economic foundations and fortuitous locations are going strong.

"The remote rural areas that are falling further and further behind have little prospect for attracting industry," said Cynthia Duncan, associate director of the Rural Economic Policy Program of the Aspen Institute, a think tank that does social and economic research. "Rural areas that are closer to cities . . . are more resilient and are going to recover faster."[37]

---

[37] http://news.google.com/newspapers?nid=1906&dat=19890805&id=VMohAAAAIBAJ&sjid=Np4FAAAAIBAJ&pg=961,4572260

Aggressive communities in Missouri and other states entice business with free land and other incentives. In Iowa, little towns struggling to pay for police protection or individual schools are banding together in "clusters" that share the costs. In Texas, the county with the largest quail population started organizing hunts that now attract hunters from 26 states.

For almost two centuries, the historical and emotional pull of rural and small-town life put the heartbeat in the heartland. The idealized myth of a homogeneous rural America, where a family lived off a bountiful land, shopped in a small town free of crime and perpetuated itself in prosperity and harmony through grit, hard work, and lofty moral principles goes back to the day the Pilgrims landed.

And yet, except for a brief "rural renaissance" in the 1970s when 4.5 million people fled the cities to earn livings in the country as coal and farming boomed, much of rural life has been on a long decline. "In the eighties," said Calvin Beale, chief Agriculture Department demographer, "we simply do not see many of the back-to-the-landers, homesteaders or urban refugees who go out to Upper Michigan, Upper Minnesota, the Ozarks, or northeastern New England to make their living in a small-town community because they prefer to do it."

The '80s added new crises to old challenges: tumbling land values, farm foreclosures, two droughts, school consolidation, falling commodity and petroleum prices, deregulation and declining services, a brain drain and a loss of jobs caused by mechanization, factory closings, and increased use of cheap Third World labor.

The result has been an exodus to urban centers and dire predictions for the future.

"Unless action is taken, virtually every citizen of the country will be forced to live in a metropolitan area," said Rep. Glenn English (D-Okla.), whose House agriculture subcommittee opened on rural development. The first hearing was in Clarksdale, Mississippi. Future hearings were scheduled for Amarillo, Texas; Marshalltown, Iowa; and Blackfoot, Idaho.

Nearly one million people left rural America in 1986-87. "That scenario is good for no one," English said. "It would overburden our cities and suburbs as much as it would devastate our rural communities."

Through the '80s, rural America has witnessed a decline in services and jobs and a rise in poverty.[38]

"You can draw a lot of parallels between remote rural areas and the inner city," said the Aspen Institute's Duncan. "In both cases, people with education and skills left. You end up without a middle class, without role models. They don't have the economic security and economic opportunity. They can't invest in the schools and good government at the local level."

---

[38] http://articles.latimes.com/1989-08-06/news/mn-193_1_rural-america

CHAPTER FIVE

Build A Team

T HE TERM "SERE" is defined as "an intermediate stage in an ecosystem prior to advancing to the point of being a climax community."[39] With the Adopt a Model™ program, SERE Administrative Services (SAS) is a matrix system deployed through a cooperative educational platform. The myriad of co-ops that deploy the ecological succession by SAS are privately owned and qualify for multiple grants—state, federal, and private. It is imperative that we understand the CO-OP Industry as a whole in our nation in order to make viable financial deployment schedules on a national level. In the SAS Adopt a Model™ we have compiled a diverse array of research to educate our readers on how co-ops can work, impact, and provide benefits to rural America.

The Cooperative model is used in a wide variety of contexts in the United States, ranging from the production

---

[39] http://en.wiktionary.org/wiki/sere

and distribution of energy, human resource, and compliance to delivery of home health care services for the elderly. Although cooperative businesses have been responsible for many market innovations and corrections of market imperfections, no comprehensive set of national-level statistics had been complied about U.S. cooperative businesses, their importance to the U.S. economy, or their impact on the lives and businesses of American citizens.

Nearly 30,000 U.S. cooperatives operate at 73,000 places of business throughout the U.S. These cooperatives own $3T in assets, and generate $500B in revenue and $25B in wages. Extrapolating from the sample to the entire population, the study estimates that cooperatives account for nearly $654B in revenue, 2M jobs, $75B in wages and benefits paid, and a total of $133.5B in value-added income.

Americans hold 350M memberships in cooperatives, which generate nearly $79B in total impact from patronage refunds and dividends. Nearly 340M of these memberships are in consumer cooperatives.

The four basic SAS cooperative measures of aggregate economic impact are: Revenue; Employment; Wages; and Income, focused on industry specific co-ops such as Commercial Sales and Marketing; Social and Public Services; Financial Services, and Utilities.

Defining the SAS Cooperative

To determine whether a given firm is a cooperative, there are five different, potential qualifying criteria: application of a statement of principles; self-identification; incorporation status; tax-filing status, and governance structure. SAS as a community development entity with principles, tax filings, and a governance structure defines the clear interpretation of a clean nine-year-old non-profit.

SAS Principles

SAS defines its character principles as a broader definition of a cooperative by the *The International Co-operative Alliance* (ICA), which employs broader terms in its definition of a cooperative as "an autonomous association of persons united voluntarily to meet their common economic, social, and cultural needs and aspirations through a jointly owned, but by consensus it is a controlled enterprise." SAS has adopted most of the Rochdale principles (based on a consumer cooperative in England, dating to 1844), five of seven worldwide. These are generally acknowledged principles that guide the cooperative enterprise: voluntary and open membership; member economic participation; autonomy and independence; education, training, and information; cooperation among cooperatives, and concern for community.

The SAS congruence between the above definitions or principles could be accessed through a close reading of its bylaws and articles of incorporation.

SAS Self-Identification

SAS is operating on a 501 (c) (3) Community Development Corporation with a deployment cooperative venue of educational platforms; however, there are no established standards for the term "cooperative" in use. Thus, SAS organizes the use of the term "cooperative" descriptively to indicate a functional approach that includes collaboration or coordination, but neither do we own nor do we control by patron members, nor do we distribute benefits based on use. SAS is not using the cooperative term as a reliable indicator of the cooperative nature of the organization.

Identifying the Structure and Use of Non-Profit Co-ops

Upwards of 85% of U.S. cooperative revenue is generated within six sectors: agriculture, the farm credit system, Federal home loan banks, rural electric service, mutual insurers and credit unions, but in recent years this has begun to change. SAS has identified the gap between big government concepts and small business impacts through its innovative Adopt a Model™ program. Historically, the cooperative model was adopted to meet the economic challenges presented by these sectors, and incorporation statutes and Federal tax provisions were developed to support these cooperatives.

Agricultural cooperatives typically incorporate under cooperative statutes, which exist in every state. They file tax returns specific to cooperative businesses, and they are also identified by the USDA Bureau of Rural Development's periodic survey of agricultural cooperatives. Rural electric cooperatives and credit unions are chartered under specific state or Federal statutes, and Federal tax exemptions were created to support these entities. Strong, active national trade associations represent both types of cooperatives, identify, and collect data on cooperatives in these sectors. Congress established the farm credit system to meet the credit needs of agriculture. Tax exemptions were created to support the system, and its nationwide network of cooperative financial institutions is well documented. SAS developed the "Adopt a Model™ " to create sustainability and position rural areas for future demand, and do it as a private company.

However, some sectors that have cooperatives do not use a single model for tax filing and incorporation. These include the SAS bio-fuels (it is not uncommon for bio-fuel cooperatives to incorporate as LLCs, for example), consumer goods, arts and crafts, and social and public services (except housing). To gain further insight into the organizational structure of cooperatives in these sectors, OCCW conducted a survey of 1,200 firms randomly sampled from the relevant population.

Table 2-1 reports variations in incorporation and tax filing status from this survey. According to Table 2-1, 80% of our sampled firms that incorporate as cooperatives choose to operate and file as either a cooperative or non-for-profit organization. In contrast, only 26% of the sampled firms that incorporate as C-corp firms file as cooperatives or not-for-profit organizations. Form 1065 is used mostly by LLCs that choose to be taxed on a "pass through" basis by electing to be taxed as partnerships.

Table 2-1 shows that a significant fraction of (15%), sampled cooperative firms choose to file a standard business 1120 form, thus forgoing the right to be taxed as a cooperative. SAS does not get taxed as a cooperative but as a 501 (c) (3) CDC non-profit even though its hybrid locations file according to state laws.

Overall, Table 2-1 clearly demonstrates potential ambiguities in identifying cooperatives in the U.S. economy solely from either incorporation or tax filing status.

Community Development Corporation 501c3 Non-profit

The SAS designation encompasses two different subsets. Incorporation statutes that are specific to cooperatives, but that classify them as non-profit entities, also make provisions for member ownership rights, including member voting rights for board of directors, distributions, and rights to residual returns.

In contrast, the SERE Administrative Services (SAS) and cooperatives incorporates under a Non-Profit Organization, qualified under I.R.C. § 501(c)(3), was founded on July 1, 2003, but general non-profit statutes are not statutorily bound to follow organizational and operational criteria specific to cooperatives, making the cooperative character for such organizations more difficult to identify. This type of non-profit cooperative frequently appears in traditional non-profit sectors such as education.

Table 2-1: Incorporation by Tax Status (Row Percentages %, N = 1,244)[1]

Incorporation Status	Sampled Firms	Percentages				
		990	990c/1120c	1120	Gov.	1065
Cooperative	806	7	73	15	5	1
C-corp	16	13	13	67	0	7
LLC[2]	51	5	5	36	0	54
Non-Profit	527	95	0	4	1	0
Other	50	11	14	54	11	11
All Cooperatives		37	43	13	3	3
SAS National %	Per State 10,000	35	55	8	2	0

Row percents add to 100. [2]Formally, a limited liability company does not "incorporate," but instead, organizes under the relevant state statute.

General non-profit statutes permit member organizations, but may not guarantee the right of members to vote. Broader statutory parameters for board selection and governance allow membership organizations to be governed by a board that is not elected or is composed of both elected and appointed directors, as well as a board elected by a one-member/one-vote system. Membership organizations incorporated under a non-profit statute may exhibit varying levels of democratic control by member patrons; whether such an organization is a cooperative is debatable, and SAS's model incorporates all sectors and organizations to accomplish the economic goals for a healthy rural America, whether republican or democratic.

The SAS cooperatives organized under general non-profit statutes that provide services may qualify for Federal tax-exempt status under IRC section 501(c)(3). This tax-exempt designation supports, among others, organizations established for educational and charitable purposes and can be a major incentive for incorporating as a non-profit. Such organizations are eligible to receive grants and tax-deductible contributions. Cooperatives organized to provide public sector-type services like the Adopt A Model™ program, are custom tailored for specialized fields that position each coop for grants and alternative funding types. It is attractive to those who live in rural America because it is an additive integration and is there to help, assist, and support.

SAS has a diverse array of cooperative venues of economic deployments. Each economic category is defined by the USDA (2006). To classify firms that did not fit within the subsectors provided by USDA categories, SAS uses the category structure created by the University of Wisconsin, which adds two new subsectoral categories:

1. **Commercial sales and marketing:** farm supply and marketing, biofuels, grocery and consumer goods retail, arts and crafts, and entertainment

2. **Social and public services:** housing, healthcare, daycare, transportation, education

3. **Financial services:** credit unions, farm credit, mutual insurance

4. **Utilities:** electric, telephone, water, and waste

SAS's cooperatives in the four sectors listed above can be considered either "producer" or "consumer" cooperatives. A producer cooperative transforms member inputs into a marketable output, while a consumer cooperative purchases wholesale goods and services to sell to its members. Additionally, SAS has "purchasing" (or business-to-business) and "worker" cooperatives that operate in a wide variety of economic sectors. Purchasing cooperatives are composed of businesses that collectively buy supplies that members use in their respective businesses. Often the businesses are retail stores that collectively purchase wholesale goods to try to establish better terms of trade. A worker cooperative is a type of producer cooperative where the input provided by members is labor.

Approximately 80% of all worker cooperatives are found in the Commercial Sales and Marketing sector (36% consumer goods retail, 9% arts and crafts, and 33% entertainment), and the remainder are found in the Social and Public Services sector (5% healthcare, 8% transportation, and 5% education).

Approximately 19% of purchasing cooperatives are found in the Commercial Sales and Marketing sector (13% grocers, and the remainder in other), 66% in Social and Public Services (21% healthcare, 44% education, and 3% transportation), 4% in the Financial Services sector (corporate credit unions), and 11% in the Utilities sector (generation and transmission cooperatives).

In the following Sections, we estimate the indirect and induced impacts that result from this economic activity, and report separately on the individual subsectors noted above and show the projected impacts SAS will have through the Adopt a Model™ program.

Figure 4-1 displays the 29,284 firms in our census by aggregate sectoral category, with each dot representing a firm's location. Within this universe, we have confirmation of individual firms to verify that patrons have both control rights and the right to residual returns in the organization (i.e., full patron ownership).

Table 4-1 summarizes economic impacts across the four aggregate economic sectors. This table is constructed by summing total economic impacts across all subsectors that constitute a given aggregate sector. For example, the Commercial Sales and Marketing aggregate sector is composed of five subsectors: agriculture, consumer goods, arts and crafts, biofuels, and other. Total impacts for each individual subsector have been constructed in five steps.

1. Discovery of the universe of firms.

2. Base data collection on a sample of firms. Core economic data includes contact information, wages (including benefits), assets, revenue, membership, patronage refunds, employment, and taxes.

3. Extrapolation of sample data to population level. When we did not have data for all firms, we used the average value for each economic indicator across all firms for which we *did* have data, multiplied by the total number of firms in the subsector. This yielded *direct* impacts.

4. Computation of *indirect* and *induced* impacts using the base data and input-output multipliers for each subsector. See our methodology appendix for details.

5. Summation of direct, indirect, and induced impacts to yield total impacts.

Accurate data for the housing sector, part of the aggregate Social and Public Services sector, could not be collected for reporting impact analysis. Adding total revenue impacts across the five sectors that make up the aggregate Commercial Sales and Marketing sector yields a total aggregate revenue of $220B and 440,198 jobs. This is produced by 3,463 firms that operate at 5,695 different places of business (establishments). Total income—a measure of value added akin to GDP for the aggregate economy—is $37B and wage impact is $13B. Financial Services is the largest aggregate sector across all measures of impact. This sector includes credit unions, the Farm Credit System, mutual insurers, and a small number of very large financial institutions that provide loan funds to cooperative businesses (or that operate on a cooperative basis with member businesses). The sector with the largest number of firms—Social and Public Services—has the smallest overall impact across all measures. Overall, 29,284 cooperatives that operate at 72,993 places of business (establishments), collectively account for nearly $652B in revenue, $154B in income, $74B in wages, and 2M jobs, not including the SAS model.

SAS is a great asset to the farming community with its Bio Fuels resources. Our Bio Fuels plants use four million bushels of corn per year and employ over a thousand year round. Our focus is with foods, nutraceuticals, and fuels. Below that we would provide the history, niche, structure, and economic impacts of the farm supply and marketing long with the bio fuels stats and the SAS financial impact results on a national deployment level.

Farm Supply and Marketing Overview

Cooperative firms account for a significant portion of economic activity in U.S. agricultural and food markets, both as providers of key inputs and as marketing and processing agents for farm output. According to USDA statistics, marketing and input supply cooperatives account for about a third of both total farm sector revenue and input purchases (USDA, 2006). Cooperatives play a key role in agricultural markets not only because they account for a significant fraction of economic activity in this sector, but also because they are believed to generate a pro-competitive effect in imperfectly competitive markets. Cooperatives play other socially beneficial roles in the agricultural sector. They provide an opportunity for farmers to share risk and to control managerial decision-making for their direct benefit. Additionally, they offer a credence attribute—farmer ownership—which can be attached to farm commodities, thus providing additional value to some consumers.

Cooperatives perform a wide variety of functions in agricultural and food markets. Often these functions are grouped into the two broad categories, "marketing" and "supply." Some marketing cooperatives are household names: Sunkist, Ocean Spray, Sun-maid, and Sunsweet, for example, have created national recognition with their branded products. These firms provide processing and marketing services to farmers, and also the necessary logistical support to aggregate farm supply. Other marketing cooperatives are much leaner organizations, providing only marketing services to assist farmers, get their product to market, to pool risk, or to negotiate sales as a group to a single buyer or a small number of buyers. Supply cooperatives provide service and inputs to farmers to help them produce their goods. Many farmers purchase basic inputs such as seed, fertilizer, and farm chemicals from a cooperative. In other words, farmers collectively establish a firm to negotiate better terms of purchase for basic agricultural production inputs. Less common, but still widely observed, are cooperatives that provide information services (e.g., record keeping and performance evaluation) to farmers.

History of Farm Co-ops

Formalization of group efforts among farmers into well-defined and legally sanctioned cooperative business organizations occurred gradually during the mid- to late nineteenth century in the U.S. Authors of early cooperative incorporation statutes modified standard stock corporation statutes to reflect Rochdale operating principles. Passage of the Sherman Antitrust Act in 1890 forced cooperative leaders to further formalize and distinguish the cooperative business model.

The Sherman Antitrust Act was designed to prevent groups of corporations from combining by granting their stock to a trust. With control of all the corporations vested in the trust board, the trust would then work to eliminate competition, create a monopoly, and thus raise prices. As independent farm businesses working together to enhance prices, farmer-marketing cooperatives were subject to prosecution under the anti-trust laws that were established as a result of the Sherman Antitrust Act. In a quest to establish a unique form of organization that would be exempt from anti-trust regulations, numerous states created new "non stock" cooperative statutes.

In addition, the Clayton Act of 1914 exempted from the Sherman Act those organizations ("agricultural or horticultural organizations instituted for the purpose of mutual help and not having capital stock or conducted for profit"). The Clayton Act created some confusion, however, because at the time many farmer cooperatives were still incorporated under older stock-based cooperative statutes.

The Capper-Volstead Act was passed in 1922 to resolve this confusion and applied broadly to associations of agricultural producers, both capital stock and non-stock associations. In addition to anti-trust exemptions, farmer cooperatives have benefited from educational and research support from the USDA and from the establishment of the Farm Credit System.

Industry Niche

Cooperatives in the agricultural sector provide basic marketing and supply services, and are more prevalent among farmers who cultivate crops than among those who raise animals (dairy being a notable exception, where cooperative firms hold a dominant market share).

Marketing and processing services are typically organized around a single commodity. Supply services are restricted to basic variable inputs—agricultural chemicals, fuel and fertilizer, seed, and crop consulting services—and operate much like a "buying group," except in the production of feed for animals. That is, farmers tend not to own the physical assets that are used to produce these inputs, but rather negotiate their purchase collectively. Less common, but still widely observed, are cooperatives that provide services (e.g., information services for record keeping, and processing services such as cotton ginning and walnut shelling). Cooperatives rarely produce farm machinery and generally are not involved in basic research to develop new production technologies.

Organizational Structure

Farmer cooperatives are typically organized under state incorporation statutes, but sometimes they are also organized as limited liability companies when a need arises for significant investment participation by individuals who do not use the firm's services.

More recently, some states have established "hybrid" LLC/cooperative statutes that sanction cooperative organizations with greater outside participation than permitted in existing cooperative statutes (but that still maintain patron control). The National Conference of Commissioners for Uniform State Law (NCCUSL) recently issued the Limited Cooperative Association Act, which is intended to provide a uniform version of hybrid statutes for potential adoption across states that do not currently have one.

Farmer cooperatives typically require all members to be active farmers. Many cooperatives provide services to non-member farmers, though incorporation statutes typically place restrictions on the amount of non-member business. Some farmer cooperatives are "open" in the sense that anyone who does business with the firm may also choose to become a member. Other farmer cooperatives are "closed" in that membership is rationed according to the availability of processing or marketing capacity.

Some farmer cooperatives elect boards of directors and make major decisions such as mergers and acquisitions or dissolution on a one-member/one-vote basis, while others make voting rights proportional to the level of service use for each member. Many farmer cooperatives proportionally "allocate" all or most earnings to patrons, but then retain up to 80% of these allocations for working capital and re-investment. Firms that operate on such a basis pay patrons for the use of their funds in future periods with a formal "equity redemption" program.

Most farmer cooperatives claim Subchapter T status for Federal tax purposes, which allows pass-through taxation. Only the patrons pay tax on earnings allocations, even if they are retained for use by the firm.

Economic Impacts

As Table 4-2 shows, we obtained data from 2,535 farmer cooperatives. Collectively, these firms account for >$40B in assets, nearly $120B in sales revenue, and pay >$6B in wages. There are approximately 2.5M farmer memberships and 150,000 employees. From Table 4-2.1, by extrapolating to the entire population (2,547 firms) and adding indirect and induced impacts to this activity, agricultural cooperatives account for nearly $130B in revenue, >200,000 jobs, $8.9B in wages paid, and >$10B in valued-added income.

Table 4-2.1: Economic Impacts for Agricultural Sales and Marketing Cooperatives

Economic Impact	Multiplier	Unit	Direct	Indirect	Induced	Total
Revenues:	1.078	Million$	119,039	4,164	5,135	128,340
Income:	1,764		6,405	2,091	2,803	11,299
Wages:	1,479		6,011	1,297	1,584	8,892
Employment:	1,425	jobs	147,708	25,261	35,579	210,548

Figure 4-2.2: Revenue and Location by County for Agricultural Cooperatives

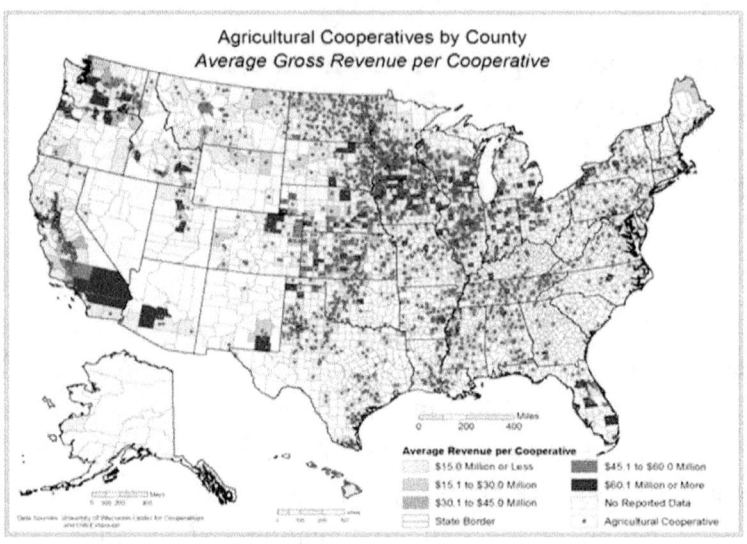

Figure 4-2.3: Employment by County for Agricultural Cooperatives

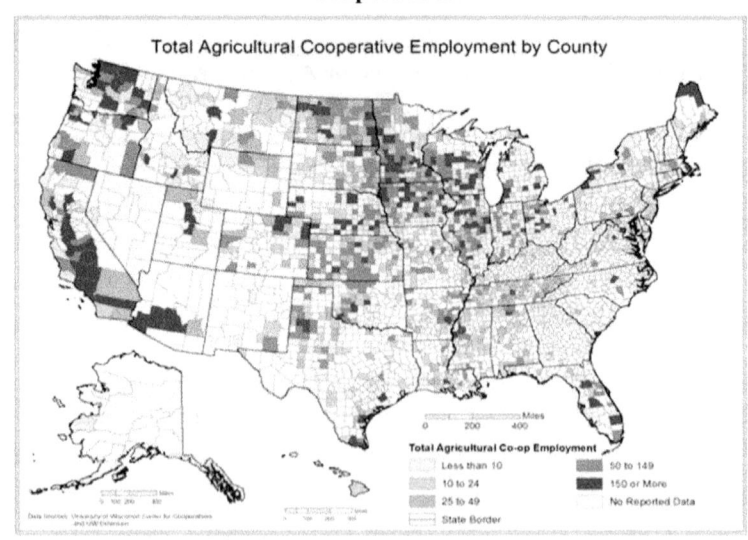

Figure 4-2.4: Membership by County for Agricultural Cooperatives

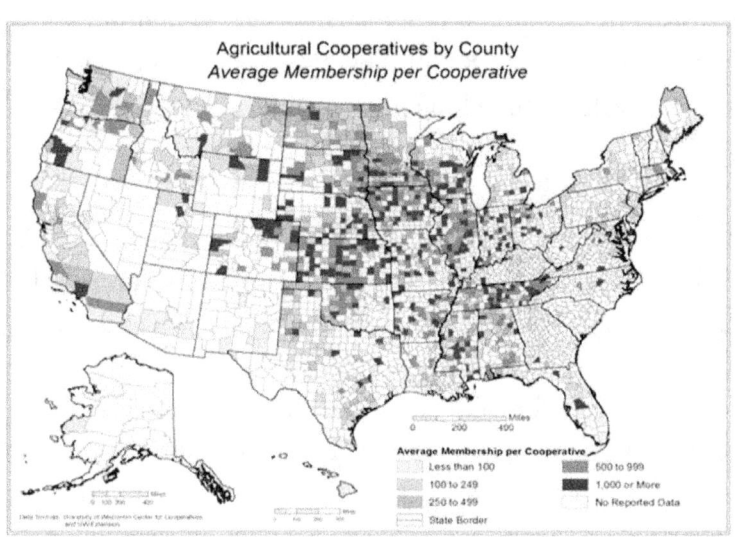

Biofuels

Biofuels cooperatives are a form of agricultural marketing cooperatives that have recently developed in response to the emerging biofuels sector of the U.S. economy. According to the Renewable Fuels Association, farmer-owned cooperatives accounted for about 15% of total production capacity in 2007, down from as much as 70-80% of total capacity in earlier years. During the massive expansion that occurred between 2004 and 2007, much of the investment capital came from private investors, rather than farmers. The data we report below came from 2007, although the entire industry is changing rapidly.

The Table 4-2 shows that 39 biofuels cooperatives collectively have close to $3B in assets. There are $4B in sales revenue, and pays $40M in wages. There are 20,000 farmer memberships and close to 2,000 employees. As shown in Table 4-2.2, by adding direct and indirect impacts to this activity, agricultural cooperatives account for >$10B in revenue, close to 8,500 jobs, $472M in wages paid, and >$1B in valued-added income.

Population Discovery and Data Sources

The sources for the business list of the thirty-nine biofuel cooperatives are the Renewable Fuels Association (RFA) and primary research. All governance data was acquired in survey work undertaken by the UWCC. The survey response rate for biofuel cooperatives is 69.5% and all reporting cooperatives provided us with 2007 fiscal year-end data. The data collection and survey methodology is discussed in detail in the Data Collection section in the Appendix.

Economic Impacts of Biofuel

As Table 4-2 shows, we have data on 17 biofuels cooperatives and these firms collectively account for >$2.8B in assets, $4.2B in sales revenue, and pay $6B in wages and benefits. There are approximately 2,000 employees and 20,000 memberships. As Table 4-2.2 shows, by extrapolating to the entire population (39 firms) and adding indirect and induced impacts to this activity, biofuels cooperatives account for close to $10B in sales revenue, >8,000 jobs, $472M in wages paid, and >$1B in valued-added income.

Table 4-2.2: Economic Impacts for Agricultural Sales and Marketing Cooperatives

Economic Impact	Multiplier	Unit	Direct	Indirect	Induced	Total
Revenues:	1.095	Million$	9,405	395	502	10,302
Income:	1.756		627	200	274	1.101
Wages:	2.445		193	124	155	472
Employment:	3.538	jobs	2,398	2,415	3,670	8,483

A new report by Bio Economic Research Associates (bio-era™), U.S. Economic Impact of Advanced Biofuels Production: Perspectives to 2030, shows that continuing to build advanced biofuels production capacity can create thousands of new jobs throughout the economy, contributing to U.S. economic growth and increasing energy security.

Biofuels may be one of the key ways to pump immediate life into the flaccid U.S. economy over the next few years, according to a new report from a research and advisory firm focused on the economics of biotechnology.

The report also states that the advanced biofuel investment could yield a direct contribution to U.S. economic growth of $37 billion by 2022, and that such investments could save a total of $350 billion in oil imports between now and 2022.[40]

---

[40] http://classic.the-scientist.com/blog/display/55481/

Figure 4-2.5: Bio-fuels Cooperative Location Map

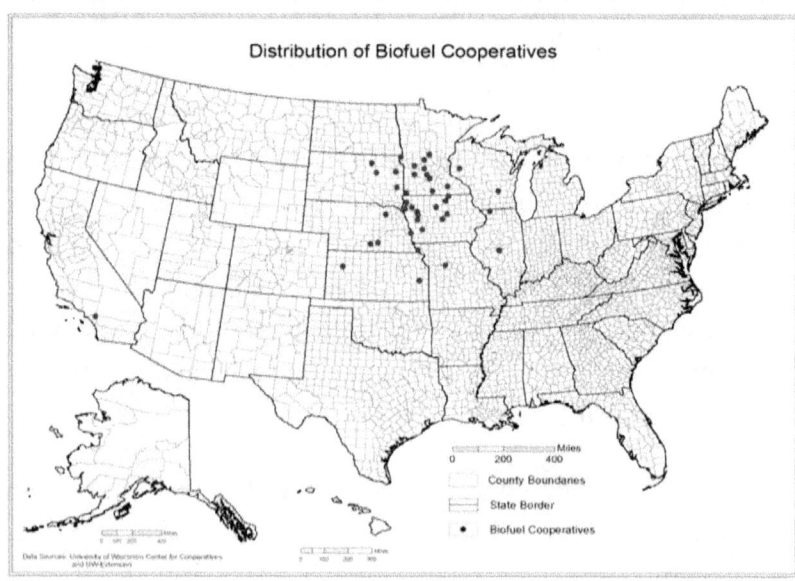

Table 4-1: Economic Impact of U.S. Cooperatives Aggregate Impacts by Sector[1]

Sector	Revenue	Income	Wages	Employment	Firms	Established
		(Million Dollars)		(Jobs)		
Commercial Sales and Marketing	201,207	37,737	13,810	422,505	3,463	5,695
Social and Public Services	7,525	2,213	1,690	424,505	11,311	11,311
Financial Services	394,363	100,661	51,176	1,133,353	9,964	50,330
Utilities	49,808	13,392	8,292	162,873	4,516	5,657
(1 Yr.) SAS by 50 States Estimate 33% Operation of 100 Bio Coops & 2,500 hybrid locations	8T	3.44T	1.92T	150,000	2,500	2,600
Total	652,903	154,002	74,969	2,143,236	29,284	72,993

[1] Analysis does not include housing cooperatives   Housing x 500 units per hybrid location @ 10K net per unit = 12T net

Housing Cooperative

A housing cooperative is formed when people join with each other on a democratic basis to own or control the housing and/or related community facilities in which they live. Usually they do this by forming a not-for-profit cooperative corporation. Each month they simply pay an amount that covers their share of the operating expenses of their cooperative corporation. Personal income tax deductions, lower turnover rates, lower real estate tax assessments (in some local areas), controlled maintenance costs, and resident participation and control are some of the benefits of choosing cooperative homeownership.

In the United States, more than 1.2 million families of all income levels live in homes owned and operated through cooperative associations.[41] People of varying needs and desires have found several ways to apply cooperative concepts in meeting their housing needs.

Cooperative housing is not a new concept. The first housing cooperative in the nation was organized in New York City in the late 1800s. Today, large numbers of housing cooperatives are located in major urban areas such as New York City, Washington, D.C., Chicago, Miami, Minneapolis, Detroit, Atlanta, and San Francisco.

SAS provides Workforce Housing, which is a term used to describe affordable housing that is developed to create home ownership opportunities for working people who

---

[41] http://www.coophousing.org/DisplayPage.aspx?id=122&bMenu=76 &bItem=122

otherwise are priced out of the housing market in the cities in which they work.

Another option is for a city to give some of their housing dollars to non-profit housing developers, with the requirement that they be used for developing ownership housing for working people in certain income ranges. These units could be reserved for specific groups such as teachers, firefighters, or nurses. Non-profits can develop these units as single family, condominiums or limited equity co-ops, but few develop these types of projects. Developing this housing as Limited Equity Housing Cooperatives guarantees permanent affordability due to built-in resale restrictions that keep the buy-in cost low for future buyers.

A third option is for a City to designate funds specifically to assist non-profits to develop co-ops. This has now become a more viable option due to recently passed legislation that allows non-profit developers to partner with labor unions or other entities to develop workforce housing for union members. AB1246 went into effect January 1, 2010, allowing unions, employers, and public entities to invest money in Limited Equity Housing Cooperatives as a way of encouraging home ownership through the development of workforce housing.

Developing Workforce Housing is a win-win proposition for cities, workers, non-profit housing developers, unions, and communities. In many states, cities are mandated to develop affordable housing and workforce housing can help cities meet their housing goals. In addition, some cities, counties, and school districts have difficulty recruiting and retaining police, firefighters, and teachers for these public sector jobs because these workers cannot afford to buy homes in the city and must commute long distances to work.

Cities are trying to shrink their carbon footprint, lower greenhouse gas emissions, reduce air pollution, and stop traffic congestion by encouraging alternative forms of transportation such as walking, buses, and bikes, and if workers could live in the same city where they work they would be much less likely to drive to work. Even more importantly, workers would have shorter commutes and could be closer to home and to their families, saving them time and money and enhancing quality of life. Workforce Housing gives unions a good return on their investment dollars, because affordable housing, and especially LEHCs, are a very sound investment in these perilous economic times. For non-profit housing developers, it provides another option for funding affordable housing in a time period where other funding sources are stretched or unavailable.

Housing cooperatives come in three basic equity structures:

- *In Market-rate housing cooperatives,* members may sell their shares in the cooperative whenever they like for whatever price the market will bear, much like any other residential property. Market-rate co-ops are very common in New York City.

- *Limited equity housing cooperatives,* which are often used by affordable housing developers, allow members to own some equity in their home, but limit the sale price of their membership share to that which they paid.

- *Group equity or Zero equity housing cooperatives* do not allow members to own equity in their residences and often have rental agreements well below market rates.

CHAPTER SIX

Go Fish

THE FAMILIAR CARD game, popular to many, called "Go Fish" is usually played among two or more players. Using a standard 52-card deck, five cards are dealt to each player—or seven if there are four or fewer. The remaining card pack is shared between the players, usually sprawled out in a non-orderly pile referenced as the "ocean" or "pool."

The player whose turn it is to play asks another player for his or her cards of a particular rank. For example, "Steve, do you have any threes?" The player who is asking must have at least one card of the rank he asked for in his hand. The recipient of the request must then hand over a card of that rank, if he or she has any. If the recipient of the request has none, he or she tells the player to "go fish," and the player draws a card from the pool and ends his turn.

When one player runs out of cards, or the pool is empty, the game ends. The player with the most piles in front of him or her wins.

When it comes to developing rural America, a vital ecosystem combines the Long Run Trend, Business Cycle, Workforce Development, multiple hybrids, various cooperatives, educational programs, and so on. However, the most important factor is money. So often, I go into a city and meet with Chambers of Commerce, business owners, and various job source and land developers. I ask them if they have capital in their region to revitalize their company. Their answer reminds me of this card game, because their answer could be summed up in two words— "Go Fish."

The era of recruiting smokestack industries and getting deep subsidies from the federal government to revitalize local economies is over. The economic future of struggling economies across the country will come from those communities themselves, based on local assets, local ideas, and driven by local entrepreneurs. To spark this growth, rural communities will need Community Development Venture Capital (CDVC) to help bring them back into the economic mainstream.

Currently, rural economies are inadequately served by venture capital. While the venture capital industry in the United States is generally very robust, rural areas have not benefited from the activity in the broader venture capital industry. The lack of the infrastructure required supporting the growth of venture capital and venture-backed companies in rural areas means rural companies generally only have limited access to sophisticated and knowledgeable consultants (lawyers, accountants, executive recruiters, and employee support services).

SERE Administrative Services (SAS) and the Adopt a Model™ program can provide a community with grant writing, cooperatives, funding with local and state WIBs, and co-ops with many venture capital groups. With the number of jobs going overseas, the opportunity of socioeconomic growth largely depends upon a knowledge-based society. The demand for jobs in technology, film, design, architectural drawings, and many other jobs is causing young people to move to urban areas.

SAS can consult a community with the proper infrastructure required to support the growth of venture capital and venture-backed companies in rural areas, since rural companies generally only have limited access to sophisticated and knowledgeable consultants (lawyers, accountants, executive recruiters, and employee support services). In spite of these obstacles, there are strong trends that point to a future where rural CDVC unleashes the energy of rural entrepreneurs. Rural areas are becoming a richer investing environment thanks to: (1) new technological breakthroughs, (2) the promise of leveraging local intellectual resources such as universities or government laboratories, and (3) "in-sourcing" of jobs from areas with higher living costs (as opposed to sending those jobs overseas).

Generally speaking, some of the greatest opportunities for venture capital investment in rural areas involve technology-based companies that are focused on overcoming infrastructure limitations. For example, the need to improve the delivery of healthcare and related services represents a wellspring of business opportunities in rural areas. Similar opportunities can be found in the need to bring broadband wireless communication and the Internet to rural communities lacking a wired infrastructure. Going one-step further, companies that are leveraging the Internet and/or wireless technology (broadband or otherwise) in rural areas are creating some compelling businesses.

SBA's Small Business Investment Company and New Markets Venture Capital programs are targeted primarily to rural America. The program provides for 300 percent leverage of private capital through the use of federally guaranteed, discounted debentures. In other words, for one dollar of private capital (called "regulatory capital") raised by a licensed RBIC, that RBIC can borrow three dollars that will be guaranteed by the USDA. The debentures are "discounted debentures" because five years of interest is deducted on a pre-paid basis, allowing the net proceeds to be invested as equity because there is not a need to generate current income to service interest payments.

Fertile the Ground

Making rural areas more fertile ground for venture capital investment will require developing a culture that is conducive to the creation and nurturing of entrepreneurs. While some might suggest entrepreneurs cannot be created, that people must be born with an entrepreneurial gene, it clearly stands to reason that communities that don't teach the concept of entrepreneurism are less likely to produce entrepreneurs. Communities that do not celebrate successful entrepreneurs or that unduly criticize those who start businesses that ultimately aren't successful are less likely to produce entrepreneurs.

Rural communities must establish entrepreneurial support and education systems. This concept goes far beyond building a "bricks-and-mortar" incubator and may not, in fact, even include the creation of facilities or buildings. Putting a person in an office building doesn't make him or her an entrepreneur any more than putting that same person in a garage makes him or her a car.

Opportunities can be found, but doing so requires a degree of sifting and searching. SAS provides fund management teams that can identify opportunities for investment. In addition, SAS recognizes the importance of developing relationships with cooperative capitalist. Because of these developed relation-ships, a venture investor in a rural setting will likely find that he must invest substantial time educating the entrepreneur in the prospective investee company about the venture capital process. Once an investment is made, the venture capitalist will likely invest time and energy introducing the company to networks of contacts that can be helpful to the company and must be committed on an ongoing basis to support the maturation of the management team, as well as future fundraising efforts.

Short-term job creation is not a substitute for long-term financial viability. At the end of the day, profit-producing, self-sustaining companies will create jobs and increase wealth in rural areas. Investors in rural-focused venture capital funds will need to invest in fund management teams that can successfully raise capital, deploy it in a manner that produces positive returns for the investors, and subsequently raise more capital. In other words, rural development venture capital funds will have to be able to execute successfully the same cycle that traditional venture funds must execute.

Ultimately, when investors are ready to make investments in rural-focused venture funds, it is imperative that those investments be made in capable and qualified management teams. Rural developmental venture capital will have a short lifespan if the management teams that are deploying the capital are not capable of producing returns that warrant continued and increasing investment by successful investors. To that end, it is critical that practitioners in the industry ensure that key legislators understand the necessity of building capacity in the ranks of rural venture fund managers, so an adequate cadre of professionally trained and experienced rural venture fund managers are available to aggregate and manage capital targeted for investment in rural areas.

Participation in the "new economy" requires an understanding of current realities. It is a truism that most new jobs in America today are created by small businesses, and entrepreneurs create small businesses. Growing small businesses and creating jobs and wealth in rural areas will require the availability of capital to be used as a tool in the hands of entrepreneurs, and the proficiency with which that tool is utilized can be improved and accelerated by including professionally managed, rural-focused venture capital funds in the process.

Our rural communities are standing at the fork in a road. One path, one of underinvestment, leads to a future that is marked by a vicious cycle of out-migration of jobs, capital,

and people. Those who are left behind will be forced to struggle in a place that is increasingly cut off from its metropolitan neighbors. Another path takes stock in the assets and ideas that all communities have and invests capital in them to generate growth, high-paying jobs, and a more viable economic future. We know rural CDCV is a tool that can help rural communities reach their economic potential. Our challenge now is to make sure all rural communities have the chance to choose the path toward economic growth.

Venture capital is an important ingredient in helping many rural entrepreneurs and communities reach their fullest economic potential. Many researchers and policymakers have concluded that insufficient equity capital in rural America impedes progress. Traditional venture capital funds do not appear to be the answer for rural America. They tend to focus on certain industries in relatively few regions of the country.

Nontraditional funds may be a way to close the rural venture capital gap. Public policy may be able to help in the building of new venture capital institutions. For instance, policymakers might expand the capital authority of current institutions. They might also use public funds to help establish investment pools or regional investment boards at new nontraditional funds. Finally, they could help form networks of funds to pool risk across regions.

Regardless of the form new rural equity funds take, policy experts and rural leaders agree that equipping rural businesses with better technology and management skills is a key to success. Linking young or beginning entrepreneurs with more experienced entrepreneurs is one effective way of improving outcomes. Policymakers, community leaders, and rural entrepreneurs both young and old have a stake in this. Each must do their part to ensure that more capital ventures into rural America.

Obstacles to Overcome

The question arises as to why it is so hard for rural places to access capital for economic development. While the underlying reasons are far from simple, a few facts are well known. First among these is that, compared to metropolitan areas, rural businesses and entrepreneurs have a smaller menu of financial products and often pay more to access capital. Furthermore, given the array of options, it is unsurprising that there is some confusion about eligibility, performance standards, requirements and the like. This is equally true whether it is a rural entrepreneur or business or a rural community.

Adding to this is increased difficulty in locating the source of some of the less well-established programs. There are many options for capital, particularly loans from state and federal sources, but rural entrepreneurs and communities are often ill equipped to identify and access these in a timely fashion. Communities may also find the application and reporting requirements for this capital difficult to manage without outside support.

Another thing that rural communities and their entrepreneurs face is competition with metropolitan areas for capital. Metropolitan areas are where the banks have their main offices, it is where the assets are, and it is increasingly where political clout is to be found. Rural areas also have fewer sources of capital competing for their business, which translates into higher costs, lower availability, and fewer options. Program rules for some economic development programs available through state and federal governments provide place-based entitlements for larger population centers, but offer only competitive grant programs for rural places.

Since venture capital is so vital to building economies regard-less of location, it is exceptionally vexing that equity investors shy away from rural places. This is, however, not perhaps too surprising. For venture capitalists, rural areas have several disadvantages. Because of rural entrepreneurs are so spread out, venture firms complain that it requires too much travel and time required to identify suitable rural investments. This lack of density makes it hard to create sufficient "deal flow" as well. Often, rural startups or expanding businesses require too much operational assistance from venture capital firms.

Rural America also abounds in the "wrong" industries for venture capital, which prefers to flow to new technologies and new industries with high rates of return. Venture firms prefer 10-year cycles with expected returns of up to 30 percent. While a high-tech future may be in the cards for some of rural America, the abundance of natural resources in rural places points to a future that capitalizes on this advantage. Unfortunately, venture capital for natural resources-based industries is very slim. Rural firms and entrepreneurs, especially those requiring significant levels of operational assistance, are unlikely to return at such high rates and short cycles.

So what does rural America need to get better access to capital for economic development? In short, we need to make sure that rural communities, entrepreneurs, and businesses have a full set of tools that is the right size for their needs, a full set of skills, and a level playing field.

Leveraging

SAS coordinates and facilitates private and foundation investment. Philanthropic investors play a major role in several states' community development financial institutions. The state is very well placed to court these organizations and connecting local institutions with state, regional, or national philanthropic organizations.

SAS builds social and human capacity in rural communities. Capital flows to people and places where the human and social capital is greatest. This can mean anything from increasing the percentage of rural residents with college education to improving the business, accounting, and marketing skills of rural entrepreneurs. Social capacity—the sum of the abilities, skills capabilities of the institutions and networks in a community—help to build and retain assets within a community. While these networks are often considered organic, the state can play an important role in bringing groups and individuals together and to facilitate the exchange of information across informal networks to create a web of support for rural communities.

SAS provides oversight and ensures accountability. Economic development activities often benefit from an outside perspective on activities and challenges. State government, and particularly the Legislature, has a role to play in setting objectives, guiding assistance, and ensuring transparency and accountability. The states with the most successful rural development programs are often characterized by a public, vocal and demonstrated commitment to addressing rural needs by state leaders.

117

SAS encourages cluster development. Cluster development has become the most commonly pursued economic development strategy. Cluster development in rural places requires new thinking about what rural places have to offer and can feasibly do. We've gotten to the point in economic development that success means to bring in something new and not adding to what is in place. The skills that the community already has should be the starting point in building economic development in order to honor what the community already has.

SAS coordinates and identifies resources. Rural communities are at a disadvantage in identifying, accessing, and managing funding from a variety of sources—state, federal, private, and philanthropic. SAS coordinates with each city by establishing central rural office/center that serves rural communities to better link with internal and external agencies and become more capable of connecting communities with opportunities.

Making it Happen

SAS works directly with Community Development Venture Capital (CDVC) groups and focuses their equity investments in underinvested markets, often in rural areas. CDVC groups provide attractive financial returns to investors and at the same time are a powerful force for economic growth and job creation. Venture capital is in short supply in rural America. Traditional venture capitalists talk privately about the "one-plane" rule: if they have to change planes to visit an investment, they are loathing to make the trip. What happens when visiting a prospective investment requires not only changing planes, but after landing also renting a car for a two-hour drive? To quantify an answer, the SAS has a direct database of businesses receiving investments from traditional venture capital funds. We found that less than one percent of the investments were made in rural areas. By comparison, our database of CDVC investments shows a much healthier level of rural investment—about the same proportion of rural to non-rural investments as the overall number of businesses in these locations.

CDVC funds focus on markets where other venture capitalists typically do not compete. Rather than participating in bidding wars for pieces of Silicon Valley high-tech firms, rural CDVC funds nurture long-term relationships with entrepreneurs in their regions. When an excellent investment opportunity arises, they have the relationship to capture the investment at a favorable valuation on attractive terms. CDVC fund managers have deep ties to their communities and markets, where they have the capacity not only to pick winning investments, but also to add significant value to investee companies. We have Venture Capital Cooperatives that sit on the boards of these companies and help with strategic planning, marketing, lining up additional financing, and anything else necessary to make the businesses in which they invest successful. After all, they are financial partners in these businesses. Traditional venture capitalist funds from outside of a CDVC fund's region are often eager to co-invest with a CDVC fund—despite the required plane change—knowing that they have a dedicated and knowledgeable local investment partner.

Investors are finding that community development venture capital funds can offer attractive financial returns and diversity for their investment portfolios. The CDVC industry is still young, so the newer, traditionally structured limited partner-ship and LLC funds have not completed their investment and harvest cycles. Early exits, however, indicate the potential for excellent financial results. A CDVC study of a portfolio of exits (including all write-offs) achieved by three older, not-for-profit, perpetual-life CDVC funds can yield a 15.5 percent internal rate of return. Higher returns may be expected from the newer, traditionally structured funds under pressure from investors to exit in a timely manner and to provide superior returns.

Unlike many workforce development agencies, SAS does not have to tread through bureaucracy, political agendas, or "red tape" to get things done, especially when it comes to community development funding. The term "community development" evokes inner-city urban communities, where community development corporations develop low-income housing and address other social needs. But the pioneers of community development venture capital are rural funds, and still many of the most experienced and accomplished CDVC funds focus on rural markets. Business development and job creation are at the heart of the rural agenda to promote economic well-being. However, in many cases, this involves smokestack chasing: state and local govern-ments luring large companies or manufacturing plants to a small community for the jobs they bring. All too often, this zero-sum strategy just moves jobs from one community to another, and job gains ultimately prove temporary, as these highly mobile companies move on to the next opportunity to take advantage of tax breaks and low wages, either in the U.S. or abroad.

By contrast, CDVC funds nurture indigenous entrepreneurs, individuals with deep roots in communities who build fast growing and lasting business enterprises tied to a local labor force. The positive-sum CDVC strategy creates permanent jobs and indigenous wealth, deeply rooted in rural communities.

By combining the efforts of grants, government funding (local, state, and federal) as well as Community Development Capital Venture groups, SAS has a greater success in accomplishing its overall strategy for developing rural America. SERE Administrative Services strength is to provide a viable ecosystem using the Adopt a Model™ strategies to create a reliable plan that maintains future demand while equipping a community with a knowledge-based society that develops multiply cooperatives and creates economic growth and long lasting sustainability.

By using Adopt a Model™ and the SAS system, rural communities no longer say, "Go Fish"—*we're out of money*. Instead, surrounding communities will be saying, "The fish are biting over there . . . let's go fishing." We can stock your pond!

TO BE CONTINUED.

Index

Adopt a Model™, vi, 13, 15, 22, 28, 29, 30, 31, 32, 36, 37, 38, 39, 42, 43, 44, 45, 48, 58, 59, 61, 62, 65, 69, 81, 84, 85, 90, 111, 123

banks, 15, 20, 51, 55, 84, 117

Bio Economic Research Associates, 101

Biofuels, 99, 101

blueprint, 29, 30, 31, 32, 34, 43, 47, 48, 49

bridge, vi, 13, 14, 15, 17, 18, 19, 21, 22, 28, 29, 52

Brooklyn Bridge, 15, 16, 18, 19, 21, 22, 31

business cycle, 22, 26, 27, 28, 69, 110

Carsey Institute, 71, 72, 76

CDVC, 110, 111, 120, 121, 122, 123

Clinton administration, 53

commodity prices, 27

communities, 14, 19, 20, 21, 22, 24, 28, 36, 37, 39, 47, 49, 64, 73, 77, 78, 79, 105, 110, 112, 113, 115, 116, 117, 118, 119, 120, 121, 122, 123

Community Development Venture Capital, 110, 120

community stakeholders, 66

Comprehensive Employment and Training Act, 52

CO-OP Industry, 81

cooperatives, 82, 83, 84, 85, 86, 88, 89, 90, 92, 93, 94, 95, 96, 97, 99, 100, 104, 106, 107, 110, 111, 123

co-ops, 60, 69, 81, 82, 105, 106, 111

cost-benefit analysis, 68

economy, vi, 14, 15, 19, 20, 22, 28, 30, 31, 33, 42, 45, 48, 51, 54, 55, 73, 82, 86, 91, 99, 101, 114

employment, 20, 21, 33, 35, 37, 53, 55, 56, 58, 61, 64, 69, 71, 91

family preservation, 42

Farm Credit System, 91, 95

financial assistance, 66

Fred Hiner, ii, iii, ix

GDP, 22, 91

Hispanic immigration, 74
housing cooperative, 104
industry, ix, 15, 19, 26, 29, 39, 41, 42, 46, 51, 55, 56, 60,
    61, 62, 66, 77, 82, 99, 110, 114, 122
information technologies, 24, 26
James Follain, 74
lenders, 20, 55
Limited Equity Housing, 105
Long-Run Trend, 69
New Markets Venture Capital, 112
non-profit, 54, 66, 83, 86, 87, 88, 105, 106
P. T. Barnum, 18
place-based strategies, 56, 59, 64, 65
President Franklin D. Roosevelt, 52
Regan administration, 52
Renewable Fuels Association, 99, 100
rural America., vi, vii, 15, 19, 24, 26, 29, 36, 37, 73, 75, 81,
    112, 116, 118, 120, 123
Rural areas, 19, 21, 77, 111, 117
rural communities, 110, 115, 119, 123
Rural Economic Policy Program, 77
SAS, 36, 38, 41, 44, 49, 54, 56, 58, 59, 60, 61, 62, 63, 64,
    65, 66, 67, 68, 69, 81, 82, 83, 84, 85, 86, 88, 89, 90, 92,
    104, 111, 113, 119, 120, 122, 123
sector-based strategies, 56, 60, 63
Small Business Investment, 112
technological innovation, 26
unions, 61, 84, 89, 90, 91, 105, 106
urban centers, 21, 79
USDA, 84, 88, 92, 95, 112
Venture Capital Cooperatives, 121
Workforce development, 55
Workforce Housing, 104, 105, 106
Workforce Investment Boards, 53, 61
Works Progress Administration, 52
Works Project Administration, 52

Notes

Notes

Notes

www.ingramcontent.com/pod-product-compliance
Lightning Source LLC
Chambersburg PA
CBHW070810180526
45168CB00002B/567